Exercises for Elite Golf Performance

Kelly Blackburn

**Fitness Consultant to
PGA TOUR Professionals**

Human Kinetics

Library of Congress Cataloging-in-Publication Data

Blackburn, Kelly, 1961-
    Exercises for elite golf performance / Kelly Blackburn.
        p.   cm.
    ISBN 0-7360-0235-9
    1. Golf--Training. 2. Exercise. I. Title.
    GV979.T68B53   1999
    796.352--dc21   99-25148
                                                                     CIP

ISBN 0-7360-0235-9

Acquisitions Editor: Martin Barnard; **Managing Editor:** Leigh LaHood; **Copyeditor:** Anne Mischakoff Heiles; **Proofreader:** Jim Burns; **Graphic Designer:** Nancy Rasmus; **Graphic Artist:** Nancy Loch; **Photo Editor:** Clark Brooks; **Cover Designer:** Jack Davis; **Photographer (cover):** Active Images/© J Blackman; **Photographer (interior):** Mil Cannon/Imagerial Film and Television; **Illustrator:** Beth Young; **Printer:** United Graphics; **Bindery:** Dekker

Human Kinetics books are available at special discounts for bulk purchase. Special editions or book excerpts can also be created to specification. For details, contact the Special Sales Manager at Human Kinetics.

Printed in the United States of America   10 9 8 7 6 5 4

Human Kinetics
Web site: www.HumanKinetics.com

United States: Human Kinetics, P.O. Box 5076, Champaign, IL 61825-5076
800-747-4457
e-mail: humank@hkusa.com

Canada: Human Kinetics, 475 Devonshire Road, Unit 100, Windsor, ON N8Y 2L5
800-465-7301 (in Canada only)
e-mail: orders@hkcanada.com

Europe: Human Kinetics, 107 Bradford Road, Stanningley
Leeds LS28 6AT, United Kingdom
+44 (0) 113 255 5665
e-mail: hk@hkeurope.com

Australia: Human Kinetics, 57A Price Avenue, Lower Mitcham, South Australia 5062
08 8277 1555
e-mail: liaw@hkaustralia.com

New Zealand: Human Kinetics, Division of Sports Distributors NZ Ltd.
P.O. Box 300 226 Albany, North Shore City, Auckland
0064 9 448 1207
e-mail: blairc@hknewz.com

contents

foreword

Strength and flexibility exercises have been a huge part of my success on the SENIOR TOUR. Since I started Kelly Blackburn's program, I have doubled my strength and tripled my flexibility. I'm stronger from the rough, and I'm driving the ball more than 20 yards farther off the tee!

When a herniated disk threatened to end my career, I avoided surgery by strengthening and stretching my upper back, neck, and shoulders. After several long weeks of rehabilitation, I returned to form and won in only my third tournament back from injury. The added strength and flexibility has been crucial to my success so far, and I look forward to playing at this level for many years to come.

I highly recommend the exercises found in *Exercises for Elite Golf Performance*. If you're willing to put in the effort and follow these programs, you're sure to see results out on the course.

Larry Nelson

fitness for golf

Advertisements bombard you these days for $800 drivers, $6 golf balls, and $100 hourly golf lessons. Yet the single most important piece of equipment you have as a golfer is your body. Your body is responsible for playing your game—the equipment isn't. And your performance suffers if the body cannot physically perform, if it is not fit. What is fitness for golf? It's about improving your golf performance, your game.

Golf requires power, strength, and finesse. The golfing athlete develops these qualities through the careful repetition of skills and painstaking attention to detail. Golf competition and techniques have advanced so greatly that just playing the game is not enough. The explosive nature of the golf swing places intense stresses on the shoulder, back, and hip joints. To prevent injury, therefore, it is important to perform stretching and strengthening exercises. The exercises in this book help condition the musculoskeletal system and reduce the risk of injuries due to the golf swing. Preseason preparation is a must for any golfer who has low levels of muscular strength and flexibility; however, it is important that a player remain *year-round* in a training regimen. Being fit for golf means your gaining longevity without developing chronic pain.

Golfers have traditionally avoided all forms of strengthening exercise for fear these would decrease movement, speed, and flexibility. Research clearly shows, however, that properly executed strength-training exercises improve body composition, increase metabolism and bone density, and reduce lower-back and arthritic pain.

Each muscle involved in the swing must be prepared and fit for performance. The rotator cuff must be strong, the abdominals must be powerful, and the legs must provide a stable base. For example, if the hip muscles lack strength, the arms and back have to compensate for them, which slows club-head speed, drains power, and can even strain the back.

Cross-training can give golfers the edge to develop these attributes. Cardiovascular and strength training provide the endurance to maintain a consistent swing for 18 holes. Injuries to the low back, shoulder, elbow, and hips are significantly reduced through a proper regimen of flexibility, cardiovascular workouts, and strength training designed to prepare the muscles for the stress of the game.

Without having regular exercise, on the other hand, a golfer finds his or her strength and agility, so vital to the game, gradually diminish. The result will be a shorter swing and loss in distance. A strong, flexible body has a greater chance to put to use whatever basic knowledge and understanding the golfer brings to the golf swing; it allows a golfer to reduce scores on the course. Being fit, in other words, is what separates the fumbling hacker from the fluid golfer.

Creating a Golf Performance Program

Pros such as Larry Nelson, David Duval, Fred Couples, Greg Norman, and Tom Lehman have improved their fitness or rebounded from serious injury to play some of the best golf of their careers. There's nothing magical in what they've accomplished: they all worked hard doing exercises just like the ones you'll find on the following pages. As you'll see, flexibility, strength and power, and endurance are the keys to better performance and lower scores.

To get results from stretching and strengthening exercises, however, you need more than just motivation to drive the ball farther than your playing partners can. The exercises should flow together in a program that's easy to follow—and easy to stick to—and that's the foundation of the Golf Performance Program.

In this chapter you have an outline of how to create an individual program. Developing your program involves using these four steps:

1. Learn the basic mechanics of the golf swing and how they relate to the body.
2. Think about your training goals and what you want to accomplish from your performance program.
3. Test your current level of fitness using the *Fitness Analyzer,* an easy-to-follow sequence of four tests, complete with scoring based on age and sex.
4. Follow the sample programs provided here in chapter 1, tailoring them to include exercises from chapters 2 through 6 as appropriate.

The end result will be a custom program, one that is tailored to your body and your goals, one that will produce the results you want!

Golf-Swing Mechanics

To get the most gains from this program you need to know the fundamental techniques of the golf swing and the parts of the body involved in golf-swing mechanics. Any type of movement involved in the golf swing (e.g., driving, chipping, putting) is delivered by muscles that lengthen or shorten across different joints of the body. The extension and contraction of muscles, along with the rotation of bones and joints, coordinate the upper and lower body to execute a swing.

The golf swing is about feel. It is how you experience the swing motion through the muscles. Muscles begin the movement, and they control the speed and accuracy of the swing. The better the muscles are trained, the more accurate the feedback you will get. Muscle movement is initiated by the brain, and the more a certain movement is repeated, the more the brain can memorize it. This "muscle memory" increases your consistency as you practice the swing and engrain the correct swing path in the mind.

Performing strength-training exercises to add power to the golf swing has proved to shorten the time it takes to relay information from the brain to the muscles. A training program for flexibility, strength, and endurance helps improve consistency of your golf swing throughout the course's 18 holes, and it retards muscle fatigue. After the age of 30, a person's muscle structure begins to degenerate; strength training therefore becomes even more important for golf enthusiasts who join the game during these later years. However, this process alone should convince younger golfers to start a fitness regimen—to assure their longevity in the game without injury.

Many golfers believe that distance results from strong arm and shoulder muscles. Although these muscles do contribute, the larger muscles of the body also are engaged. (See figure 1.1 for a diagram of the muscles discussed here.) The leg's abductors, adductors, and extensors move the hip backward and straighten it. The hip initiates the downswing, and at impact it is the driving force behind the ball. Strengthening the hip muscles and using the hip effectively during the swing relates to your gaining distance off the tee.

Still other muscles beyond the arms and shoulders play important roles. The abdominals are used at address for correct posture and protection of the low back. The neck flexors come into play to tilt the head forward. The pectoralis major (in the chest) is activated to pull the arms in front of the body. The elbow extensors straighten the arms, and muscles of the wrists and hands afford a good grip of the club.

Turning attention to the backswing, this stroke is initiated by the hip abductor while the knee flexors are still in a bent position but are starting to rotate. The hip flexor moves the opposite hip forward, and the external obliques turn the torso. The knee flexors (hamstrings) bend both knees slightly, while the ankle flexors are used to place both feet in the correct stance. The rotator cuffs turn the shoulders backward, whereas the biceps and triceps rotate the arms and assist in protecting the shoulder joint during the backswing. The trapezius turns the left shoulder blade outward, while the latissimus dorsi swings the right arm backward. The elbow flexor bends the right elbow slightly, and the wrist flexors bend both wrists.

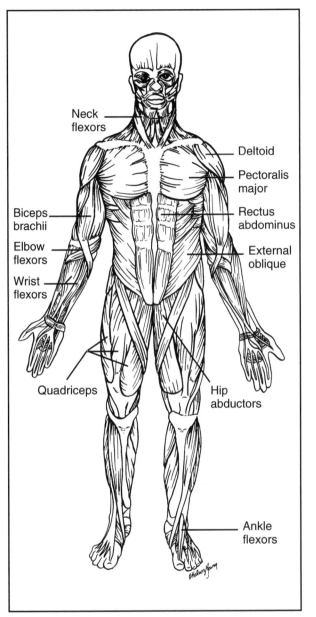
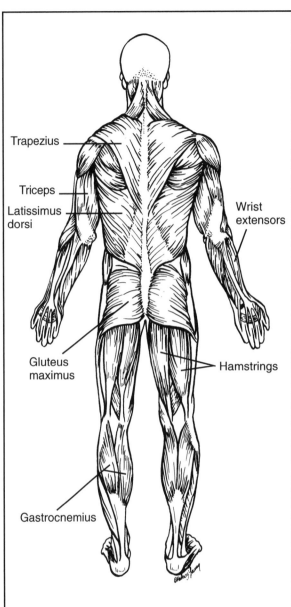

Figure 1.1   Front and back views of the human muscular structure.

During the downswing the muscle action is reversed. During the follow-through the muscles used in the backswing repeat the same action for the opposite side of the body. In all, a balanced action equally involving both sides of the body creates the golf swing.

The coiling of the upper body while the lower body resists, along with the power of the downswing and follow-through, can wreak havoc on a golfer's back. It is the number-one injury seen in both amateurs and touring professionals. Muscles twist and pull at the lumbar spine. If the player has poor posture or poor abdominal strength and is inflexible, the spine's discs are susceptible to being pressed during the swing, resulting in lower-back pain. Strength training gives the muscles surrounding the spine the power to cushion the blow at impact. Strength-training exercises also retard the brittleness of bones that comes with age.

Golf Performance Goals

The Golf Performance Programs are set up along two main goal paths: (1) strength and power and (2) endurance. And since flexibility is so important, stretching exercises also are included: they are a foundation for all the programs. Read through the following sections and choose which path is more important to you. Then take the tests found in the Fitness Analyzer. Your test scores will direct you toward the correct path according to your areas of greatest need.

Flexibility for Golf

Flexibility is vital to the game of golf. The prestretch prepares the body for the stress of the game and aids in preventing injuries. The poststretch enhances the golfer's range of motion for a fuller, more efficient shoulder turn.

The *static stretching techniques,* which this guide emphasizes, quickly produce dramatic improvements in the range of motion for the player. However, by using *partner techniques* you can move further into the stretch position, producing still greater range of motion. One other method favored for maximum gains in flexibility is the *proprioceptive neuromuscular facilitation* (PNF) method (see chapter 6). While this technique increases benefits to golfers, it also increases the risk of injury, so work slowly when you use the PNF method.

Strength and Power for Golf

Machines and free weights are great aids for increasing strength safely and effectively. The keys to safety are having proper form and using the appropriate speed for each exercise. Studies show that free weights are more versatile and convenient, while machines are less risky since the weight is balanced. So use both types of weights, if they're available, to add variety to the workout and prevent boredom.

To maximize your effectiveness in the golf swing, you must use the entire body. Because of this fact, each muscle group of the body must be trained equally. An efficient golf swing creates less stress on the back and, therefore, less risk of the injuries associated with the golf swing. *Over*activity in one particular region or part of the body, in contrast, can

- increase the risk of injury because there are increased demands or stresses on the region,
- cause inconsistency because an awkward and unbalanced swing will not be the same twice, and
- make likely an improper and inefficient swing, which wastes time and energy.

Endurance for Golf

Golf is good exercise if you walk and carry your golf bag. To avoid shoulder stress when you carry the bag, however, it is wise to use a double strap on the bag to balance the clubs. This allows the weight of the clubs to be balanced, and it helps eliminate additional lower-back strain.

It is not good for players to ride in a cart. Sitting and compressing the spine between shots adds to lower-back irritation. It is better to walk to keep the muscles warm and supple during the round. If necessary you can use a pull cart for the clubs. Although golf is not an aerobic exercise, it does burn more than 200 calories per hour. If you walk and carry your clubs for 18 holes, over the four to five hours you will be using 800-plus calories.

A golf course adds up to impressive mileage. For example, a course that is 6,100 yards adds up to more than three miles. Encourage yourself to walk in order to boost your fitness level while playing the game you love!

Cardiovascular training gives you the edge to play 18 consistent holes. Many players experience a decline in endurance at hole 13. Training a minimum of two days weekly using an interval format will boost your game and energy level. Use as many different types of cardiovascular training as possible to prevent boredom and challenge the body. Unless you're accustomed to regular running or jogging, don't start this kind of aggressive training because it can stress the hips, knees, and back. If you are interested in starting a jogging program, take it slowly and seek out the advice of a professional to make sure you stay healthy and injury-free. Keeping these areas healthy and strong is important to your game.

The elliptical trainer, treadmill, Stairclimber, recumbent bike, step training, ski machine, and rowing machine are just a few good examples to choose from. Program the recommended duration according to the fitness level you have, using the interval format. Monitor yourself or have a coach or friend help monitor you frequently to ensure there is not a drop below 65 percent of the maximum heart rate. Watch closely during the anaerobic portion to ensure the heart rate does not exceed 100 percent of maximum for more than 90 seconds!

Tracking Your Goals

The following list summarizes the types of goals you should be thinking of when developing your Golf Performance Program. Record your goals on paper, and review this list from time to time. Adjust your workouts when you have finished a program or when your goals have changed.

- **Improve flexibility.** Injuries to the key muscle groups used in the golf swing can be significantly lowered by improving flexibility. Proper stretching prepares the body for the stress of the game and improves overall range of motion.
- **Add general strength.** Strength training increases overall flexibility in those muscles supporting the joints involved in the full swing.
- **Strengthen the rotator cuff.** Strengthening the shoulder girdle increases stability at the top of the backswing position.
- **Strengthen the abdominals.** Powerful abdominals improve posture at the address and help to prevent lower-back pain associated with the golf swing.
- **Strengthen muscles of the upper legs.** Strengthening the upper legs provides improved balance during the swing.
- **Strengthen muscles of the hips.** Strengthening the hips adds power and club-head speed.
- **Strengthen muscles of the lower legs.** Strong calf muscles add push-off power in the downswing.

- **Strengthen muscles of the trunk.** A strong lower back is critical to making an effective turning motion in the golf swing.
- **Strengthen muscles of the forearms, wrists, and hands.** Strengthening the forearms, wrists, and hands adds to better club control.
- **Strengthen muscles of the upper arms.** Strong biceps and triceps muscles are vital for golf performance. Triceps are important for distance off the tee.
- **Increase cardiovascular capacity.** Increased aerobic capacity enhances endurance, which helps to maintain your consistency in playing over 18 holes.

Fitness Analyzer

The Fitness Analyzer is designed to help you determine your fitness level. The following four tests measure flexibility, upper-body strength, trunk strength, and lower-body strength. Each activity will be scored as follows: Level I = 1 point, Level II = 2 points, and Level III = 3 points. Total the points upon completion and match your score to the fitness ranking chart on page 12. Warm up and stretch before attempting these tests.

FITNESS ANALYZER

Test #1 Flexibility

◀ Sit upright on the ground or floor with the legs extended in front and the feet slightly apart. Place a yardstick between the feet with the 15-inch mark at the heels. Place one hand atop the other and lean forward from the waist as far as possible.

▶ Do not bounce or jerk. The number on the ruler that is at the top of the middle finger indicates your flexibility. Match the number of inches you reach to the chart given here to assess your current status.

Men's Score by Age in Years					
	20-29	30-39	40-49	50-59	60+
Level III	19+	18+	17+	16+	15+
Level II	13-18	18+	17+	10-15	9-14
Level I	10-12	12-17	11-16	7-9	6-8

Women's Score by Age in Years					
	20-29	30-39	40-49	50-59	60+
Level III	22+	21+	20+	19+	18+
Level II	16-21	15-20	14-19	13-18	18+
Level I	13-15	12-14	11-13	10-12	12-17

FITNESS ANALYZER

Test #2 Upper-Body Strength

◀ From a modified position, do as many push-ups as possible in a 60-second period.

▶ Match the number of push-ups you achieve to the appropriate chart to assess your current status.

Women's Score by Age in Years					
	20-29	**30-39**	**40-49**	**50-59**	**60+**
Level III	33+	34+	28+	23+	21+
Level II	23-32	22-33	18-27	15-22	13-20
Level I	12-22	10-21	8-17	7-14	5-12

FITNESS ANALYZER

Test #2 Upper-Body Strength *(continued)*

◀ From a military position, do as many push-ups as possible in a 60-second period.

▶ Match the number of push-ups you achieve to the appropriate chart to assess your current status.

Men's Score by Age in Years					
	20-29	**30-39**	**40-49**	**50-59**	**60+**
Level III	43+	37+	31+	28+	27+
Level II	30-42	25-36	21-30	18-27	17-26
Level I	17-29	13-24	11-20	9-17	6-16

FITNESS ANALYZER

Test #3 Torso Strength

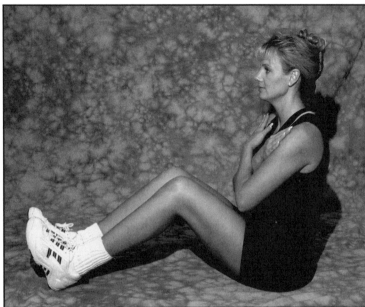

◄ Sit on the floor with the knees bent and the heels on the floor. Place the arms across the chest.

▶ Slowly lower the torso to a 45-degree angle. Maintain this angle for as long as possible. Match the number of seconds you hold the angle to this chart to assess your current status.

Male and Female Rating	
Level III	25+
Level II	15-24
Level I	5-14

FITNESS ANALYZER

Test #4 Lower-Body Strength

Place the back against the wall, with the feet 18 inches away from the wall. Bend the knees and lower the torso until the hips are just above a right angle. Maintain this angle for as long as possible. Match the number of seconds you hold the position to the chart to assess your current status.

Male and Female Rating	
Level III	90+ seconds
Level II	60-89 seconds
Level I	30-59 seconds

Fitness Ranking

To calculate your overall fitness ranking, add up your scores (or levels) from the four tests and compare the total to the chart below. For example, Tom, a 54-year-old male, reached 12 inches in test #1, completed 30 push-ups in test #2, held a 45-degree torso angle for 15 seconds in test #3, and kept a 90-degree lower-body angle for 74 seconds in test #4. Tom therefore scored 2, 3, 2, and 2 for a total score of 9, which means that he should begin the program at Level II.

4-7 total points scored = Level I	
Cardiovascular duration:	10-20 minutes
Free weight range:	0-5 pounds
Plate loading range:	10-50 pounds
Number of repetitions:	8-10

8-11 total points scored = Level II	
Cardiovascular duration:	20-30 minutes
Free weight range:	5-8 pounds
Plate loading range:	20-60 pounds
Number of repetitions:	10-12

12 or more total points scored = Level III	
Cardiovascular duration:	30-45 minutes
Free weight range:	8-15 pounds
Plate loading range:	30 + pounds
Number of repetitions:	12-15

Building a Program

This is a year-round training regimen. It is essential that you continue to practice and play while the body grows accustomed to the workout. Recover for a minimum of two hours before heading to the driving range. Please remember to be careful and not push too hard in the beginning. It works better in the long run that you *ease* into the program—the one situation you want to avoid is being too sore to play or practice following a workout! The exercises are supposed to help your golf, not hinder your time on the course.

Once you have determined your fitness level using the Fitness Analyzer, start incorporating flexibility, strength, and endurance exercises a minimum of four days each week. Flexibility exercises should be done pre- and postworkout—

and after warm-up and cooldown periods. The poststretch can be done with a partner or using the proprioceptive neuromuscular facilitation (PNF) method (see chapter 6).

Strength exercises should be done using a 2-2-4 format or 2-2 format as noted. A 2-2-4 format involves two counts initiating the exercise to the maximum position, two counts holding the maximum position while flexed, and four counts emphasizing negative resistance returning to the start position. A 2-2 format is for the exercises that have a constant movement: two counts on the initiation and two counts for the return to the start position. Each exercise should be done in succession with no rest between. Once the first muscle group is completed, stretch the next muscle group before moving on. Move fluidly through each exercise. Try listening to music with a tempo at about 124-130 beats per minute—this should help you with the correct timing for the exercises. (To order music that works well for this purpose, call 1-800-315-2329.)

Do cardiovascular training for endurance using an *interval format* for a sustained period of time (see pages 14 and 15 for a recommended duration). This approach emphasizes both aerobic and anaerobic training, which are equally important in golf. You need to be able to recover quickly from walking up steep hills on the course, for example, and the best way to improve your recovery is through aerobic and anaerobic training. Work at a minimum of 65 percent of your maximum heart rate (220 bpm minus your age = maximum). You can reach close to your maximum during anaerobic training, but don't hold this level of exertion longer than approximately 90 seconds.

Sample Programs

After determining the results from your performing the Fitness Analyzer, follow the appropriate level of program as indicated on pages 14 and 15. Both the strength and power program and the endurance program contain flexibility exercises that will help to maximize your gains.

Here is a checklist of equipment you'll need:

1. Step bench with risers
2. Ankle weights in pairs, including 10 and 20 pounds
3. Hand weights in pairs, including 3, 5, 8, 10, 12, 15 pounds
4. Abdominal roller
5. Floor mat
6. Music (optional)

STRENGTH PROGRAMS

Level I

Strength and Power for Golf	2 days weekly minimum
Warm-Up	5 minutes
Prestretch: Flexibility for Preparation and Prevention	10 minutes
Strength Exercises: Power for Golf	32 minutes
Poststretch: Improving Range of Motion	20 minutes

Endurance for Golf	2 days weekly minimum
Warm-Up	5 minutes
Prestretch: Flexibility for Preparation and Prevention	10 minutes
Cardiovascular: Endurance for Golf	20 minutes
Cooldown	5 minutes
Poststretch: Improving Range of Motion	20 minutes

Level II

Strength and Power for Golf	2 days weekly minimum
Warm-Up	5 minutes
Prestretch: Flexibility for Preparation and Prevention	10 minutes
Strength Exercises: Power for Golf	40 minutes
Poststretch: Improving Range of Motion	20 minutes

STRENGTH PROGRAMS

Level II
continued

Endurance for Golf	2 days weekly minimum
Warm-Up	5 minutes
Prestretch: Flexibility for Preparation and Prevention	10 minutes
Cardiovascular: Endurance for Golf	30 minutes
Cooldown	5 minutes
Poststretch: Improving Range of Motion	20 minutes

Level III

Strength and Power for Golf	2 days weekly minimum
Warm-Up	5 minutes
Prestretch: Flexibility for Preparation and Prevention	10 minutes
Strength Exercises: Power for Golf	48 minutes
Poststretch: Improving Range of Motion	20 minutes

Endurance for Golf	2 days weekly minimum
Warm-Up	5 minutes
Prestretch: Flexibility for Preparation and Prevention	10 minutes
Cardiovascular: Endurance for Golf	45 minutes
Cooldown	5 minutes
Poststretch: Improving Range of Motion	20 minutes

The individual exercises are found in the next five chapters. Whatever your level, you should go through the stretches in chapter 2 to select exercises for the prestretch and poststretch phase for each program. Recommended prestretch routine: exercises 2, 4, 6 ,7, 8, 11, 12, 13, 15, 17, 18, 19, 20, 22, 25. Recommended poststretch routine: exercises 1, 3, 5, 9, 10, 14, 16, 21, 23, 24, 26, 27, 28, 29.

The strength chapters are organized by program level: if you tested at Level I, go to chapter 3; Level II means you should go to chapter 4; and for Level III you should go to chapter 5. The partner-assisted stretches and strength exercises in chapter 6 can benefit golfers at all levels.

Follow the guidelines in each chapter closely to choose the appropriate exercises for your program level. Once you have completed the program, retest yourself using the Fitness Analyzer to see if you should move on to the next level. Don't despair if your progress comes gradually—you can remain within the range of the same level for many months. Keep working; the long-term gains are worth it!

Developing a More Flexible Swing

Now that you know your fitness level, the next step is to select specific stretches from this chapter to make up your prestretch and poststretch routine. Flexibility exercises will prepare your body for the stresses found in the golf swing and will help prevent injuries.

Each stretch should be done slowly, in a controlled manner emphasizing technique. Once you obtain a comfortable stretch position, hold the stretch without bouncing for the recommended number of seconds.

Once you have finished your round, don't forget your poststretch routine. Working your muscles while they are still warm and supple will increase your long-term range of motion. Repeat each exercise and try to stretch the muscles slightly farther each time you repeat.

①TILT STRETCH

Stand with feet shoulder-width apart, or sit on a bench or in a chair. Sit upright, flexing the abdominal muscles to support the back. Slowly drop the head toward the right shoulder.

Return to the start position and repeat the motion to the opposite side.

PRESTRETCH: Hold for 10 seconds on each side.

POSTSTRETCH: Hold for 10 seconds on each side and repeat.

> **TIP**   To prepare the neck muscles for the impact of the golf swing, try stretches 1, 2, or 3. Do not strain; remain relaxed, and do not lift the shoulder.

2 SIDE STRETCH

NECK MUSCLES

Stand with feet shoulder-width apart, or sit on a bench or in a chair. Sit upright, flexing the abdominal muscles to support the back. Slowly turn the head to the right. Gently push against the chin for a good stretch.

Return to the start position and repeat to the opposite side.

PRESTRETCH: Hold for 10 seconds on each side.

POSTSTRETCH: Hold for 10 seconds on each side and repeat.

TIP   Do not strain; keep the torso facing forward.

3 REAR STRETCH

NECK MUSCLES

Stand with feet shoulder-width apart, or sit on a bench or in a chair. Sit upright, flexing the abdominal muscles to support the back. Place the hands behind the head and slowly drop the head forward.

Gently apply downward pressure for a good stretch. Return to the start position.

PRESTRETCH: Hold for 10 seconds.
POSTSTRETCH: Hold for 10 seconds and repeat.

TIP Do not roll the shoulders forward.

4 TRICEPS STRETCH

ARM AND SHOULDER MUSCLES

Stand with feet shoulder-width apart, or sit on a bench or in a chair. Sit up-right, flexing the abdominal muscles to support the back. Extend one arm overhead.

Bend the extended arm, and slowly drop down with the palm facing forward.

Hold the bent elbow with the opposite hand and gently pull back to create the stretch. Return to the start position and repeat to the opposite side.

PRESTRETCH: Hold for 10 seconds on each side.

POSTSTRETCH: Hold for 10 seconds on each side and repeat.

TIP Stretches 4, 5, 6, 7, and 8 extend range of motion in the arms to get the club deep in the backswing. Remember to keep the head and torso upright.

5 RIB CAGE STRETCH

ARM AND SHOULDER MUSCLES

Sit on a bench or in a chair. Sit upright, flexing the abdominal muscles to support the back. Extend the arms upward and press the palms together as shown.

Stretch the arms up and slightly backward. Inhale and lift; exhale and relax.

PRESTRETCH: Hold for 10 seconds.

POSTSTRETCH: Hold for 10 seconds and repeat.

TIP Keep the head and neck relaxed.

6 BACK OF SHOULDER STRETCH

ARM AND SHOULDER MUSCLES

Kneel on the ground or sit on a bench or in a chair. Sit upright, flexing the abdominal muscles to support the back. Interlace the fingers above the head.

With the palms facing downward, gently push the arms back and up.

PRESTRETCH: Hold for 10 seconds.

POSTSTRETCH: Hold for 10 seconds and repeat.

TIP   Do not arch the back.

7 FRONT OF SHOULDER AND CHEST STRETCH

ARM AND SHOULDER MUSCLES

Stand with the feet shoulder-width apart and the toes straight ahead. Extend the arms down and back, interlacing the fingers. Inhale and slowly expand the chest.

To accelerate this stretch, lift the arms upward.

PRESTRETCH: Hold for 10 seconds.

POSTSTRETCH: Hold for 10 seconds and repeat.

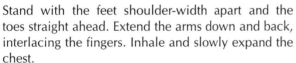

TIP Do not arch the back.

8 MIDBACK STRETCH

ARM AND SHOULDER MUSCLES

Stand with feet shoulder-width apart, or sit on a bench or in a chair. Sit upright, flexing the abdominal muscles to support the back.

Gently pull one elbow across the chest toward the opposite shoulder. Return to the start position and repeat for the opposite side.

PRESTRETCH: Hold for 10 seconds on each side.

POSTSTRETCH: Hold for 10 seconds on each side and repeat.

TIP Keep the torso facing forward and the bent arm parallel to the floor.

9 UPPER-BACK STRETCH

FINGER, HAND, WRIST, SHOULDER MUSCLES

Kneel on the ground or sit on a bench or in a chair. Sit upright, flexing the abdominal muscles to support the back. Interlace the fingers out in front at shoulder height. Turn the palms outward.

Slowly round the back to feel the stretch.

PRESTRETCH: Hold for 10 seconds.

POSTSTRETCH: Hold for 10 seconds and repeat.

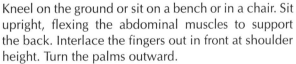

TIP To prepare the fingers, hands, wrists, and shoulders for the force of the golf swing, perform stretches 9 and 10.

10 HIP STRETCH

HIP MUSCLES

Stand with your feet shoulder-width apart and your toes pointed slightly outward. Keeping your knees slightly bent, place one hand on your hip for support. Extend the opposite arm up and over your head.

Slowly bend at your waist to the side opposite the extended arm. When you feel a good stretch hold this position. Return to the start position and repeat to the opposite side.

PRESTRETCH: Hold for 10 seconds on each side.
POSTSTRETCH: Hold for 10 seconds on each side and repeat.

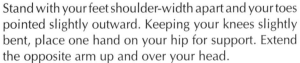
TIP   Do not tilt your hip outward.

11 ROTATION STRETCH

UPPER-TRUNK MUSCLES

Stand with your feet shoulder-width apart and with your arms extended in front of you at shoulder height. Your toes should point slightly outward.

Slowly turn your upper body as far as possible with only minimal turn in your hips. Return to the start position and repeat to the opposite side.

PRESTRETCH: Hold for 15 seconds on each side.

POSTSTRETCH: Hold for 15 seconds on each side and repeat.

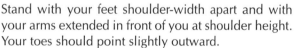

TIP For a fuller backswing, increase upper trunk flexibility with this stretch. Do not force yourself to turn beyond a comfortable point.

12 CALF AND ACHILLES STRETCH

LOWER-LEG MUSCLES

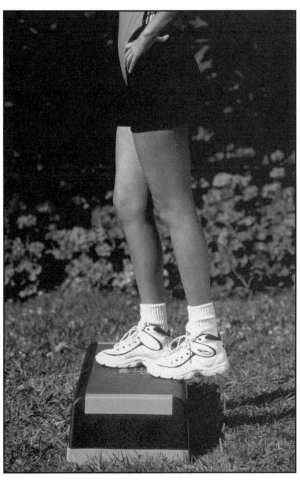

Stand atop an elevated platform with your toes pointed straight ahead. Move one foot to the back of the platform until the ball of your foot is at the edge.

Bend the knee of the front leg and slowly lower your heel to create the stretch in your calf. Bend the knee of the lowered leg to create a stretch in your Achilles tendon. Return to the start position and repeat to the opposite side.

PRESTRETCH: Hold both the calf and Achilles tendon for 15 seconds on each side.

POSTSTRETCH: Hold for 15 seconds on each side and repeat.

| TIP | Add push-off power in your downswing by increasing lower-leg flexibility with stretches 12 and 13. |

13 SHIN STRETCH

LOWER-LEG MUSCLES

Place your heel atop an elevated platform with your toe pointed upward. Slightly bend the knee of the opposite leg and place both hands at the top of your thighs for balance.

Slowly lower the toe of the foot that is elevated until you feel a good stretch in the shin. Return to the start position and repeat to the opposite side.

PRESTRETCH: Hold for 15 seconds on each side.
POSTSTRETCH: Hold for 15 seconds on each side and repeat.

14 PRAY STRETCH

SHOULDER, ARM, AND BACK MUSCLES

◀ Position yourself on your hands and knees. Reach forward with your hands 12 to 14 inches, keeping your palms on the ground.

▶ Slowly pull back while you press downward with your palms. Let your chest drop slightly toward the floor to accelerate the stretch. Return to the start position.

PRESTRETCH: Hold for 10 seconds.

POSTSTRETCH: Hold for 10 seconds and repeat.

TIP Use stretches 14, 15, and 16 to prepare the shoulders, arms, and back for the impact of the golf swing. Do not sit back on your knees.

15 CAT STRETCH

SHOULDER, ARM, AND BACK MUSCLES

◀ Position yourself on your hands and knees.

▶ Slowly round your back upward until you feel a good stretch. Return to the start position. Inhale as you lift; exhale as you return.

PRESTRETCH: Hold for 10 seconds.

POSTSTRETCH: Hold for 10 seconds and repeat.

TIP Return to the start position slowly.

16 LATS AND BACK STRETCH

SHOULDER, ARM, AND BACK MUSCLES

Position yourself on your hands and knees.

Place your hands to one side, reaching away from the body with the outward arm, and slowly rotate your torso creating the stretch. Return to the start position and repeat to the opposite side.

PRESTRETCH: Hold for 10 seconds on each side.

POSTSTRETCH: Hold for 10 seconds on each side and repeat.

TIP   Keep your hips stationary; do not tilt them outward.

17 BICEPS, FOREARMS, AND WRISTS STRETCH

ARM MUSCLES

◀ Position yourself on your hands and knees. Slowly rotate your wrists until your thumbs are pointed to the outside, with your fingers pointed toward your knees.

▶ Keeping your palms flat, lean back until you feel a good stretch. Return to the start position.

PRESTRETCH: Hold for 10 seconds.

POSTSTRETCH: Hold for 10 seconds and repeat.

TIP   Add flexibility to the arms for better club control with this stretch.

18 FRONT HIP STRETCH

HIP MUSCLES

◀ Begin on your knees; move one leg forward until the ankle of the forward leg is extended slightly beyond the knee.

▶ Lean forward and lower the front of your hip downward to create the stretch. Return to the start position and repeat to the opposite side.

PRESTRETCH: Hold for 20 seconds on each side.

POSTSTRETCH: Hold for 20 seconds on each side and repeat.

TIP If you are experiencing low back pain associated with the golf swing, use stretches 18 and 19, which also increase hip turn. If you have knee problems, do this stretch slowly and carefully.

19 HAMSTRINGS STRETCH

HIP AND LOWER-BACK MUSCLES

Sit on the floor or ground with your legs straight, your feet upright, and your legs no more than six inches apart. Bend from the waist and reach forward to create the stretch. Return to the start position.

PRESTRETCH: Hold for 15 seconds.
POSTSTRETCH: Hold for 15 seconds and repeat.

20 STANDING QUADS STRETCH

HIP AND UPPER-LEG MUSCLES

Stand with your feet slightly apart and both knees slightly bent.

Lift one lower leg and hold the top of your foot between the toe and ankle joint. Pull the heel toward the buttock. Contract the buttock and push your hip forward (and downward) to accelerate the stretch. Return to the start position and repeat on the opposite side.

PRESTRETCH: Hold for 15 seconds on each side.

POSTSTRETCH: Hold for 15 seconds on each side and repeat.

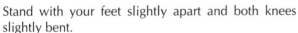 **TIP** Use stretches 20 and 21 to improve flexibility and balance during the golf swing. Place a chair in front of you for assisted balance.

21 LYING QUADS STRETCH

HIP AND UPPER-LEG MUSCLES

◀ Lie on one side and extend your arm (rest your head on it).

▶ Bend the knee of your top leg and hold the top of that foot between the toe and ankle joint. Gently pull the heel toward the buttock. Contract the buttock and push the hip forward to create the stretch. Return to the start position and repeat to the opposite side.

PRESTRETCH: Hold for 15 seconds on each side.

POSTSTRETCH: Hold for 15 seconds on each side and repeat.

22 LOWER-BACK STRETCH

SPINE

◀ Lie on your back with your knees bent and the feet flat on the floor.

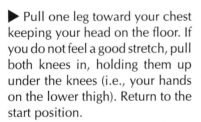

▶ Pull one leg toward your chest keeping your head on the floor. If you do not feel a good stretch, pull both knees in, holding them up under the knees (i.e., your hands on the lower thigh). Return to the start position.

PRESTRETCH: Hold for 10 seconds.

POSTSTRETCH: Hold for 10 seconds and repeat.

TIP Stretches 22, 23, and 24 loosen the spine to promote a fuller turn on the backswing.

23 LOWER-HIP STRETCH

SPINE

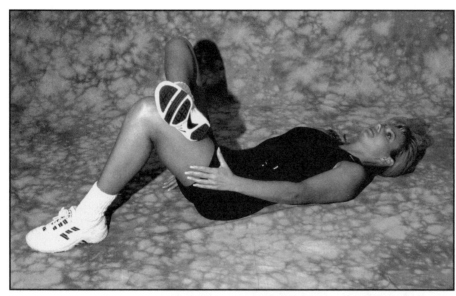

◀ Lie on your back with your knees bent and feet flat on the floor. Cross one leg over the knee of the opposite leg, placing your ankle just above the knee.

▶ Place both hands around your thigh and slowly lift the bottom leg until you feel a good stretch. Return to the start position and repeat to the opposite side.

PRESTRETCH: Hold for 15 seconds on each side.
POSTSTRETCH: Hold for 15 seconds on each side and repeat.

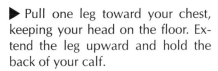

HIP AND THIGH STRETCH

◀ Lie on your back with your knees bent and feet flat on the floor.

▶ Pull one leg toward your chest, keeping your head on the floor. Extend the leg upward and hold the back of your calf.

◀ Extend the opposite leg to create both the hip and thigh stretch. Return to the start position and repeat to the opposite side.

PRESTRETCH: Hold for 20 seconds on each side.

POSTSTRETCH: Hold for 20 seconds on each side and repeat.

27 GROIN STRETCH

INNER-THIGH MUSCLES

Lie on your back with your knees bent. Place your hands on the outside of your thighs. Slowly lower your legs and place the soles of your feet together. Let the pull of gravity do the stretching.

To accelerate the stretch press downward on your upper thighs. Return to the start position.

PRESTRETCH: Hold for 20 seconds.
POSTSTRETCH: Hold for 20 seconds and repeat.

28 ABS AND ANKLES STRETCH

ABDOMINAL AND ANKLE MUSCLES

◀ Lie on your back with your arms at your sides.

▶ Extend the arms overhead and straighten the legs. Reach as far as you can in opposite directions with your arms and legs (point your toes and extend your fingers) until you feel a good stretch. Return to the start position.

PRESTRETCH: Hold for 10 seconds.
POSTSTRETCH: Hold for 10 seconds and repeat.

29 ABS AND LOWER-BACK STRETCH

ABDOMINAL AND LOWER-BACK MUSCLES

◀ Lie facedown with your arms close to your side and your palms flat on the floor.

▶ Slowly press upward until you feel a good stretch. Return to the start position.

PRESTRETCH: Hold for 10 seconds.

POSTSTRETCH: Hold for 10 seconds and repeat.

TIP Do not lift your hips from the floor and do not strain the lower back.

Strength Level I: Building a Base

The goal in Level I is to get your muscles accustomed to lifting weights and to develop a base level of strength on which you can build. Stick with it—you'll be amazed at how much stronger you feel after just a few short weeks. Look through the exercises in the chapter and select one from each muscle group. The total amount of exercise time for Level I is 32 minutes. If you fall short of the target exercise time, feel free to add exercises for muscles you feel need the most work. (To determine which areas need more work, review your scores on the Fitness Analyzer, and concentrate on the areas in which you scored low.) Refer back to the recommended weight ranges and reps on page 12.

Technique is especially important at this stage because you are conditioning your muscles and tendons to respond to the load placed upon them. You want to condition your muscles the right way, so pay close attention to the form in the exercise photos. Keep your prestretch and poststretch routines handy for the beginning and the end of your workout. Monitor yourself to ensure that you are breathing correctly; always exhale during the exertion of each exercise.

30 BEGINNER LUNGE

UPPER-LEG MUSCLES

Stand with one foot atop the platform. Place the opposite foot flat on the floor and place the hands on the hips. Stand with the feet at a natural width apart and the back straight. Position both feet so that the toes point straight ahead.

Bend the knee of the back leg and dip the knee downward while lifting the heel. Flex the quadriceps muscle, hold for a two-second count, and slowly rise to the start position as you press through the heel of the front foot. Repeat up to 10 reps. Do the same for the opposite side.

TIP Strengthen your upper legs for a more stable base and improved balance with exercises 30-33. Focus your eyes on some point straight ahead of you to help maintain your balance.

31 BEGINNER SQUAT

UPPER-LEG MUSCLES

Stand with the feet shoulder-width apart and place both hands on the hips.

Descend to a squatting position, keeping the knees directly above the toes. Squat to a 45-degree bend in the knees. Hold for a two-second count and slowly rise to the start position as you press through the heels while flexing the buttocks and quadriceps muscles. Repeat up to 10 reps.

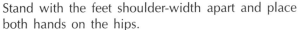

TIP Keep the head up; do not lean forward.

32 SKI SQUAT

UPPER-LEG MUSCLES

Stand with the feet slightly apart, and place both hands on the hips.

Slowly descend to a squatting position, keeping the knees directly above the toes. Squat to a 45-degree bend in the knees. Hold for a two-second count and slowly rise to the start position as you press through the heels while flexing the buttocks and quadriceps muscles. Repeat up to 10 reps.

TIP Keep the head up; do not lean forward.

33 GLUTEAL PROPULSION

UPPER-LEG MUSCLES

◀ Stand with one foot atop the platform and toes pointing straight ahead. Use the foot atop the platform to propel upward.

◀ Lift the opposite leg backward and upward while flexing the foot and gluteal muscles. Hold for a two-second count and return to the start position, but avoid placing the heel on the floor.

▶ Balance on the toes and bend the knee. Repeat up to 10 reps. Do the same for the opposite side.

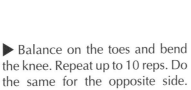

TIP Focus your eyes on some point straight ahead to help maintain balance. This exercise should be controlled with no hesitation between reps (use the 2-2 format).

34 STRAIGHT CALF

LOWER-LEG MUSCLES

Stand in the center of the platform (use no risers) with the toes pointing straight ahead. Move both feet back until the heels are off the platform, and place the hands on the hips.

Raise both heels as high as possible, flexing the calf muscles. Hold for a two-second count and slowly return to the start position. Repeat up to 10 reps.

TIP Use this exercise to add push-off power in the downswing. Do not bounce or drop rapidly back to the start position. Do not let the ankles roll out. Focus your eyes on some point straight ahead to prevent losing your balance. Place a chair in front of the platform for assisted balance.

35 GLUTEAL LIFT

HIP MUSCLES

◀ Place the elbows atop the platform, grip the front of the platform, and place both knees on the floor.

▶ Raise one leg and bend it at the knee to form an L-shape. Flex the foot, buttock, and hamstrings muscles.

◀ Lift the leg and unbend the knee slightly. Hold for a two-second count and return to the start position. Repeat up to 10 reps. Do the same for the opposite side.

TIP Exercises 35-39 strengthen the hips for more power and clubhead speed. Do not arch the back. Maintain a good head position by looking at the back of the hands, which keeps the head parallel to the body (use the 2-2 format).

36 ADDUCTOR SQUAT

HIP MUSCLES

Stand with the feet more than shoulder-width apart and hands on the hips.

Descend to a squatting position, a 45-degree bend in the knees and still keeping the knees directly above the toes. Hold for a two-second count and slowly rise to the start position, pressing through the heels while flexing the gluteal and adductor muscles. Repeat up to 10 reps.

TIP Keep the head up; do not lean forward.

37 ADDUCTOR LIFT

HIP MUSCLES

◀ Lie on one side with the chest and hips pressed against the platform step. Extend the lower arm to rest the head on it. Place the upper leg atop the platform with the knee bent to form a right angle. Straighten the lower leg and flex the foot.

▶ Lift the lower leg as high as possible, flexing the adductor muscle. Hold for a two-second count and slowly return to the start position. Repeat up to 10 reps. Do the same for the opposite side.

TIP Do not let the foot rest on the floor.

38 STANDING ABDUCTOR RAISE

HIP MUSCLES

Stand with the feet slightly apart and place your hands on the hips.

Flex the gluteals and slowly extend one leg to the side, raising it four to six inches off the floor. Hold for a two-second count and return to the start position. Repeat up to 10 reps. Do the same for the opposite side.

TIP Do not arch the back or swing the leg upward. Keep the torso upright, and do not tilt the hips outward. Keep the knees slightly bent at all times. Place a chair in front of you for assisted balance. Use the 2-2 format.

39 LYING LIFT

HIP MUSCLES

◀ Lie with the back on the floor, knees bent, heels on the floor, and toes upward.

▶ Flexing the gluteals, press the adductors together and lift the hips. Hold for a two-second count and slowly return to the start position. Do not let the hips rest on the floor. Repeat up to 10 reps.

TIP Do not arch the back. **Recommendation:** You may feel the need to stretch before continuing. If so, repeat stretches 18, 19, and 21.

40 ALTERNATE LOWER-BODY PRONE LIFT

BACK MUSCLES

◄ Lie facedown with the legs extended and the arms bent and close to the rib cage for support.

► Flex the gluteals and lift one leg as high as possible, keeping it straight. Hold for a two-second count and return to the start position. Do not let the foot rest on the floor. Repeat up to 10 reps. Do the same for the opposite side.

TIP To increase turn and prevent low back strain, use exercises 40, 41, and 42. Keep the lower back relaxed and do not arch it.

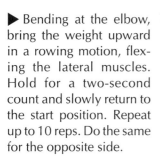

KNEELING BENT ROW

BACK MUSCLES

◀ Kneel with one knee on a bench and place one hand at the end of the bench for support. Holding a dumbbell in the opposite hand, extend the arm and angle the dumbbell so that the top head is in line with the supporting hand.

▶ Bending at the elbow, bring the weight upward in a rowing motion, flexing the lateral muscles. Hold for a two-second count and slowly return to the start position. Repeat up to 10 reps. Do the same for the opposite side.

TIP Keep the back flat and the head in a neutral position. If you have knee problems, substitute exercise 42.

42 BENT-BACK ROW

BACK MUSCLES

Stand with one foot atop the platform. Hold a dumbbell in the hand opposite from the foot atop the platform. Bend at the waist and place the empty hand (not holding the dumbbell) just above the knee. Extend the arm holding the dumbbell and angle it so that the bottom head is in line with the toe atop the platform.

Bending at the elbow, bring the weight upward in a rowing motion, flexing the lateral muscles. Hold for a two-second count and slowly return to the start position. Repeat up to 10 reps. Do the same for the opposite side.

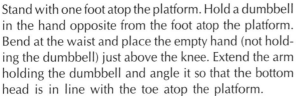

TIP Do not arch the back. **Recommendation:** You may feel the need to stretch before continuing. If so, repeat stretches 8 and 22.

43 ALTERNATE BICEPS CURL

UPPER-ARM AND SHOULDER MUSCLES

◀ Stand with the feet slightly apart and a dumbbell in each hand. Extend the arms down and place the elbows close to the rib cage.

◀ Flex the biceps and curl one arm upward toward the shoulder. As the weight approaches the shoulder, flex the opposite bicep and begin curling the opposite arm.

▶ Lower the weight that began curling first as the opposite arm ascends (use the 2-2 format). Repeat up to 10 reps for each side.

TIP   For added distance off the tee, use exercises 43, 44, and 45 to strengthen the upper arms and shoulders. Do not arch the back or make a rocking motion as you lift and lower the weight.

44 FLAT CROSS EXTENSION

UPPER-ARM AND SHOULDER MUSCLES

◄ Lie faceup on the platform, with knees bent and both feet on the floor. Hold a dumbbell in one hand and extend that arm up with the palm facing away from the body.

▶ Bending the elbow, lower the weight to the opposite shoulder. Flex the triceps muscle and slowly return to the start position. Hold for a two-second count and repeat. Repeat up to 10 reps. Do the same for the opposite side.

TIP Do not swing the arm, and keep the elbow pointing upward at all times.

45 REVERSE EXTENSION

UPPER-ARM AND SHOULDER MUSCLES

◀ Lie faceup on the platform with knees bent and both feet on the floor. Hold a dumbbell with both hands gripping the outside heads of the dumbbell. Extend both arms upward and back over the head slightly.

▶ Bending the elbows, lower the weight behind the head. Flex the triceps muscle and slowly return to the start position. Hold for a two-second count and repeat up to 10 times.

TIP Do not swing the arms, and keep the elbows pointing upward at all times. **Recommendation:** You may feel the need to stretch before continuing. If so, repeat stretches 4 and 17.

46 ALTERNATE SHOULDER LATERALS

SHOULDER MUSCLES

◀ Stand with the feet shoulder-width apart. Holding a dumbell in each hand, extend your arms down.

◀ Lift one arm upward in front to shoulder height. As the weight approaches shoulder height, begin lifting the opposite arm.

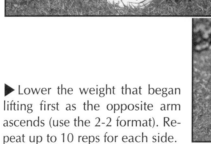
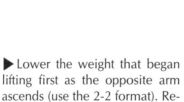

▶ Lower the weight that began lifting first as the opposite arm ascends (use the 2-2 format). Repeat up to 10 reps for each side.

TIP Use exercises 46 and 47 to strengthen the shoulders for more stability at the top of the backswing. Do not arch the back or make a rocking motion as you lift and lower the weight.

47 SEATED SHOULDER LATERALS

SHOULDER MUSCLES

Sit on a bench with the feet on the floor. Hold a dumbbell in each hand and extend the arms down at the sides.

Raise both arms upward to the sides until the wrists are just above shoulder height. Hold for a two-second count and slowly return to the start position. Repeat up to 10 reps.

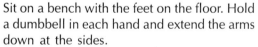

TIP Do not arch the back.

48 ELEVATED MODIFIED PUSH-UPS

CHEST MUSCLES

◀ Place the hands atop the platform, shoulder-width apart; place the knees on the floor, and elevate the lower legs. Tilt the torso forward until the shoulders, torso, and buttocks (in a straight line) form an approximate 45-degree angle to the ground.

◀ Lower the torso toward the platform. Hold for a two-second count and slowly return to the start position flexing the pectoral muscles. Repeat up to 10 reps.

TIP To maximize effectiveness in the golf swing, perform exercises 48-51. Keep the head in a neutral position and do not arch the back.

49 ELEVATED MILITARY PUSH-UPS

CHEST MUSCLES

◀ Place both hands atop the platform, shoulder-width apart, and extend both legs back.

▶ Lower the torso toward the platform. Hold for a two-second count and slowly return to the start position, flexing the pectoral muscles. Repeat up to 10 reps.

TIP   Keep the head in a neutral position and do not arch the back.

50 FLAT CHEST PRESS

CHEST MUSCLES

◄ Lie faceup on the platform with knees bent and both feet on the floor. Hold a dumbbell in each hand and extend the arms upward.

► Flex the pectoral muscles and slowly lower the weight until the elbows are just below parallel to the platform. Hold for a two-second count and slowly return to the start position. Repeat up to 10 reps.

TIP   Relax the grip during motion and do not arch the back while lifting.

51 FLAT CHEST FLY

CHEST MUSCLES

◀ Lie faceup on the platform with knees bent and both feet on the floor. Hold a dumbbell in each hand and extend the arms upward. Bend the elbows slightly as though hugging a barrel.

▶ Flex the pectoral muscles and slowly lower the weight out and down until the elbows are just below parallel to the platform. Hold for a two-second count and slowly return to the start position. Repeat up to 10 reps.

TIP   Relax the grip during the motion; do not arch the back while lifting. **Recommendation:** You may feel the need to stretch before continuing. If so, repeat stretches 6 and 7.

52 LOWER-ABS LIFT

ABDOMINAL MUSCLES

Using the risers, raise the platform to an incline position. Lie faceup on the floor, placing the buttocks at the end of the platform. Place both legs atop the platform and place the hands under the buttocks extending the arms toward the feet until the lower back is felt on the floor. Contract the abdomen and lift both legs until the body forms a right angle. Slowly lower to the start position, but do not let the legs rest atop the platform. Hold for a two-second count and repeat up to 10 reps.

TIP Strengthen your abdominals to improve posture at address with exercises 52, 53, and 54. Do this exercise in a slow and controlled manner. Do not swing the legs.

53 ABS CROSSOVER

ABDOMINAL MUSCLES

◀ Lie back with both knees bent and both feet on the floor. Place one ankle over the opposite knee, and lift the toe of the opposite leg. Support the neck by placing the hand opposite the leg you crossed behind your head. Extend the opposite arm to the side of the body.

▶ Contract the abdomen and slowly raise the shoulder and upper back. Turn slightly, aiming the shoulder toward the knee of the crossed leg. Hold for a two-second count and then return to the start position. Repeat up to 10 reps. Do the same for the opposite side.

TIP Keep the elbow in line with the head at all times.

54 ASSISTED ABDOMINAL CRUNCH

ABDOMINAL MUSCLES

◀ Lie back on the floor with both knees bent and the toes pointing upward. Rest the head and arms on the ab roller.

▶ Contract the abdominal muscles and slowly curl upward until the shoulders are off the floor. Hold for a two-second count and then return to the start position. Repeat up to 10 reps.

Strength Level II: Adding Strength and Power

Whether you've graduated from Level I or you're starting out at this stage, the goal in Level II is to build on your base of strength. The exercise time is longer—40 minutes—and you'll be adding more weight throughout the program (refer back to page 12 for guidelines). If you begin this level and experience difficulty with the weight recommendations on page 12, feel free to go back to Level I. Starting at the right level is the safest, most effective way to get results.

As in Level I remember to stretch for 10 minutes pre-workout, and 20 minutes post-workout to increase your range of motion. Perform each exercise quickly and efficiently by paying close attention to the technique featured in the exercise photographs; always exhale during the exertion phase of each exercise.

57 SEATED LEG EXTENSION

UPPER-LEG MUSCLES

◀ Wrap each ankle with a 5- or 10-lb. ankle weight. Sit on the end of the bench, with the feet flat on the floor.

▶ Flex the foot and quadriceps (upper thigh). Raise the leg until it is parallel to the floor. Hold for a two-second count and slowly return to the start position. Repeat up to 12 reps. Do the same for the opposite side.

TIP   Keep the back upright; do not arch it during the motion.

58 SPLIT SQUAT

UPPER-LEG MUSCLES

Stand in the center of the platform, facing one end, with the arms extended forward.

Step wide off the center of the platform, placing the foot on the floor with the toes facing slightly away from the step. Bend both knees, lower the hips behind the heels, and place 75 percent of the weight on the foot that is on the floor. Lower the body to a 45-degree bend in the knee atop the platform. Contract the gluteals and quadriceps and spring back to the start position, pressing through the heels. Repeat up to 12 reps, using the 2-2 format. Do the same for the opposite side.

TIP Focus your eyes on some point straight ahead to help maintain your balance. Keep the head up and the motion fluid.

59 ANGLED-OUT CALF RAISE

LOWER-LEG MUSCLES

◀ Wrap each ankle with a 5- or 10-lb. ankle weight. Stand in the center of the platform (use no risers) with the toes angled out and the heels approximately six inches apart. Move both feet back until the heels are off the platform; place the hands on the hips.

▶ Raise both heels as high as possible, flexing the calf muscles. Hold for a two-second count and slowly return to the start position. Repeat up to 12 reps.

TIP Use this exercise to add push-off power in the downswing. Do not bounce or drop rapidly back to the start position. Do not let the ankles roll out. Focus your eyes on some point straight ahead to prevent losing your balance. Place a chair in front of the platform for assisted balance.

60 LYING LEG CURL

HIP MUSCLES

◀ Wrap each ankle with a 5- or 10-lb. ankle weight. Lie facedown on the bench with the knees off the end. Flex both feet and contract the gluteals. Press the ankles, knees, and inner thighs together.

▶ Bending the knees, raise the legs until a right angle is formed. Hold for a two-second count and slowly return to the start position. Repeat up to 12 reps.

TIP Exercises 60, 61, and 62 strengthen the hips for more power and clubhead speed. Do not swing the legs or arch the back during the motion.

61 INTERMEDIATE ADDUCTOR SQUAT

HIP MUSCLES

Stand with the feet more than shoulder-width apart. Hold a dumbbell with both hands between the legs.

Descend to a squatting position, with a 45-degree bend in the knees but still keeping the knees directly above the toes. Hold for a two-second count and slowly rise to the start position, pressing through the heels while contracting the gluteal and flexing adductor muscles. Repeat up to 12 reps.

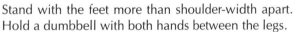

TIP Keep the head up; do not lean forward.

62 EXTENDED ABDUCTOR LIFT

HIP MUSCLES

◀ Wrap each ankle with a 5- or 10-lb. ankle weight. Lie on one side with both legs extended. Extend the arm and rest the head on it. Flex the foot and contract the gluteal muscle of the upper leg.

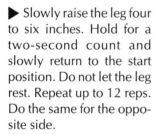

▶ Slowly raise the leg four to six inches. Hold for a two-second count and slowly return to the start position. Do not let the leg rest. Repeat up to 12 reps. Do the same for the opposite side.

TIP Keep the toe and knee forward at all times. **Recommendation:** You may feel the need to stretch before continuing. If so, repeat stretches 18, 19, and 21.

63 COMBINATION PRONE LIFT

BACK MUSCLES

◀ Lie facedown with the legs extended, one arm bent close to the rib cage for support and the other arm extended. Contract the gluteals of the leg opposite the extended arm.

▶ Lift this flexed or contracted leg and opposite arm as high as possible, keeping both straight. Hold for a two-second count and slowly return to the start position. Do not let the foot or hand rest on the floor. Repeat up to 12 reps. Do the same for the opposite side.

TIP To increase turn and prevent low back strain, perform exercises 63, 64, and 65. Keep the lower back relaxed.

64 SIMULTANEOUS LOWER-BODY PRONE LIFT

BACK MUSCLES

◀ Lie facedown with the legs extended and the arms bent and close to the rib cage for support.

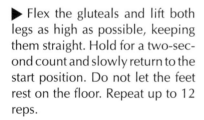

▶ Flex the gluteals and lift both legs as high as possible, keeping them straight. Hold for a two-second count and slowly return to the start position. Do not let the feet rest on the floor. Repeat up to 12 reps.

TIP Keep the lower back relaxed. Let the legs split a natural width during the motion.

65 UPRIGHT ROW

BACK MUSCLES

Stand with the feet shoulder-width apart. Hold a dumbbell in each hand and extend the arms in front.

Flex the upper back and raise both arms, leading with the elbows, to just above the chest. Hold for a two-second count and slowly return to the start position. Repeat up to 12 reps.

TIP Keep the weights close to the body. Do not arch the back during the motion.

66 HAMMER BICEPS CURL

UPPER-ARM MUSCLES

◀ Sit on the end of the bench with both feet flat on the floor. Hold a dumbbell in each hand and extend the arms down to the side.

◀ Keeping the weight in a "hammer" position, flex the biceps and curl one arm upward toward the shoulder.

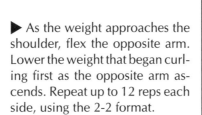

▶ As the weight approaches the shoulder, flex the opposite arm. Lower the weight that began curling first as the opposite arm ascends. Repeat up to 12 reps each side, using the 2-2 format.

TIP For added distance off the tee, use exercises 66-69 to strengthen the upper arms and shoulders. Make sure not to arch the back.

67 OVERHEAD TRICEPS EXTENSION

UPPER-ARM MUSCLES

Sit on a bench or in a chair with both feet flat on the floor. Hold a dumbbell by cupping one end. Extend the arms overhead.

Bending at the elbows, lower the weight down behind the head. Contract (flex) the triceps muscles and slowly return to the start position. Hold for a two-second count. Repeat up to 12 reps.

TIP Do not swing the arms or arch the back.

68 KNEELING TRICEPS EXTENSION

UPPER-ARM MUSCLES

◀ Kneel on the bench and place one hand at the end of the bench for support. Holding a dumbbell in the opposite hand, bend the arm upward, positioning the elbow just above waist height.

▶ Flex the triceps muscle and extend the arm back. Hold for a two-second count and slowly return to the start position. Repeat up to 12 reps. Do the same for the opposite side.

TIP Keep the back flat and the head in a neutral position. Do not swing the arm. If you have knee problems, substitute exercise 69.

69 TRICEPS KICKBACK

UPPER-ARM MUSCLES

Stand with one foot atop the platform. Hold a dumbbell in the other hand, opposite from the foot atop the platform. Bend at the waist and place the hand without the dumbbell just above the knee. Bend the arm holding the weight upward, positioning the elbow close to the waist and back slightly.

Flex the triceps muscle and extend the arm back. Hold for a two-second count and slowly return to the start position. Repeat up to 12 reps. Do the same for the opposite side.

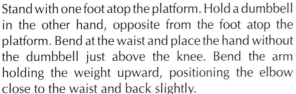

TIP Do not arch the back. **Recommendation:** You may feel the need to stretch before continuing. If so, repeat stretche s 4 and 17.

70 SIMULTANEOUS FRONT LATERALS

SHOULDER MUSCLES

Stand with the feet shoulder-width apart. Hold a dumb-bell in each hand, with the arms extended down.

Lift both arms upward in front to shoulder height. Hold for a two-second count and slowly return to the start position. Repeat up to 12 reps.

TIP Use exercises 70, 71, and 72 to strengthen the shoulders for more stability at the top of the backswing. Do not arch the back or make a rocking motion as you lift and lower the weight.

71 SHOULDER SHRUG

SHOULDER MUSCLES

◀ Sit on the end of the bench or in a chair with both feet flat on the floor. Hold a dumbbell in each hand and extend the arms to the side.

◀ Lift the shoulders upward as high as possible. Hold for a two-second count.

▶ Return to the start position by drawing the letter C backwards. Repeat up to 12 reps.

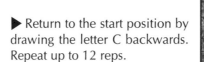

TIP The weight serves as an anchor. Do not lift the arms while raising the shoulders.

72 PEE-WEE LATERAL

SHOULDER MUSCLES

Sit at one end of the bench with the feet in a straddled position. Holding a dumbbell in each hand, place the arms behind the back with the heads of the weights together.

Raise the arms outward and upward until the wrists are just above shoulder height. Hold for a two-second count and slowly return to the start position. Repeat for 12 reps.

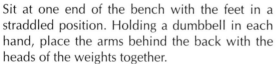

TIP Do not arch the back during the motion.

73 MODIFIED PUSH-UPS

CHEST MUSCLES

◀ Place the hands on the floor, shoulder-width apart; place the knees on the floor, and elevate the lower legs. Tilt the torso forward until the shoulders, torso, and buttocks (in a straight line) form a 45-degree angle with the floor.

▶ Lower the torso toward the floor. Hold for a two-second count and slowly return to the start position, flexing the pectoral muscles. Repeat up to 12 reps.

TIP To maximize effectiveness in the golf swing, perform exercises 73, 74, and 75. Keep the head in a neutral position and do not arch the back.

74 MILITARY PUSH-UPS

CHEST MUSCLES

◀ Place the hands on the floor, shoulder-width apart, and extend both legs back.

▶ Lower the torso toward the floor. Hold for a two-second count and slowly return to the start position, flexing the pectoral muscles. Repeat up to 12 reps.

TIP Keep the head in a neutral position and do not arch the back.

75 INCLINE CHEST PRESS

CHEST MUSCLES

Using the risers, elevate the platform to an inclined position. Lie faceup on the bench with both feet on the floor. Holding a dumbbell in each hand, extend the arms upward.

Flex (contract) the pectoral muscles and slowly lower the weights until the elbows are just below parallel to the bench. Hold for a two-second count and slowly return to the start position. Repeat up to 12 reps.

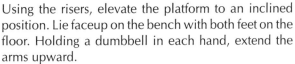

TIP Relax the grip during motion and do not arch the back while lifting. **Recommendation:** You may feel the need to stretch before continuing. If so, repeat stretches 6 and 7.

76 REVERSE ABS CURL

ABDOMINAL MUSCLES

Lie back on the floor with both legs extended upward, ankles crossed, and hands behind the head.

Flex (contract) the abdominal muscles and lift the hips upward. Slowly return to the start position. Repeat up to 12 reps, using the 2-2 format.

TIP To improve posture at address, strengthen the abdominals with exercises 76, 77, and 78. Do not swing the legs.

77 ASSISTED OBLIQUE

ABDOMINAL MUSCLES

◀ Lie back on the floor with both knees bent and the feet flat on the floor. Rest the head and arms on the abs roller. Lower the knees to one side.

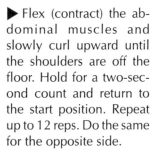

▶ Flex (contract) the abdominal muscles and slowly curl upward until the shoulders are off the floor. Hold for a two-second count and return to the start position. Repeat up to 12 reps. Do the same for the opposite side.

78 ELEVATED ABDOMINAL CRUNCH
ABDOMINAL MUSCLES

◀ Lie back on the floor with both knees bent and your heels atop the platform. Support the neck by placing both hands behind the head.

▶ Flex the abdominal muscles and slowly curl upward until the shoulders are off the floor. Hold for a two-second count and then return to the start position. Repeat up to 12 reps.

TIP   Keep the elbows in line with the head at all times.

Strength Level III: Maximizing Your Gains

If you've tested at Level III or have graduated from Level II, you're ready to maximize strength and power in the golf swing. Start with one exercise for each muscle group, then add more exercises until you reach the target exercise time of 48 minutes. Again, remember to include the warm-up, prestretch and poststretch routines.

Focus on technique and work all the major muscle groups. Increase the weight once you reach 15 repetitions (refer to page 12), and experiment by adding new exercises to your routine. As in the previous program levels, always exhale during the exertion of each exercise.

79 ADVANCED LUNGE

UPPER-LEG MUSCLES

◀ Stand with your feet together a comfortable distance from the step. Holding a dumbbell in each hand, extend the arms down.

◀ Extend one foot forward, placing it atop the platform. At the same time bend the knee of the opposite leg.

▶ Moving in a downward motion, lift the heel of the opposite leg. Spring back to the start position by pressing through the heel of the front foot. Repeat up to 15 reps, using the 2-2 format. Do the same for the opposite side.

TIP Strengthen your upper legs for a more stable base and improved balance with exercises 79, 80, and 81. Focus your eyes on some point straight ahead of you to help maintain your balance.

80 ADVANCED SQUAT

UPPER-LEG MUSCLES

Stand with the feet shoulder-width apart. Hold a dumbbell in each hand and rest them on the shoulders.

Descend to a squatting position, keeping the knees directly above the toes. Squat to a 45-degree bend in the knees. Hold for a two-second count and slowly rise to the start position as you press through the heels while flexing the buttocks and quadriceps muscles. Repeat up to 15 reps.

TIP   Keep the head up; do not lean forward.

81 ADVANCED SKI SQUAT

UPPER-LEG MUSCLES

Stand with the feet slightly apart. Hold a dumbbell in each hand and rest them on the shoulders.

Descend to a squatting position, keeping the knees directly above the toes. Squat to a 45-degree bend in the knees. Hold for a two-second count and slowly rise to the start position as you press through the heels while flexing the buttocks and quadriceps muscles. Repeat up to 15 reps.

TIP Keep the head up; do not lean forward.

82 ANGLED-IN CALF RAISE

LOWER-LEG MUSCLES

◀ Wrap each ankle with a 5- or 10-lb. ankle weight. Stand in the center of the platform (use no risers), with the toes angled in and the feet approximately six inches apart. Move both feet back until the heels are off the platform; place the hands on the hips.

▶ Raise both heels as high as possible, flexing the calf muscles. Hold for a two-second count and slowly return to the start position. Repeat up to 15 reps.

TIP Use this exercise to add push-off power in the downswing. Do not bounce or drop rapidly back to the start position. Do not let the ankles roll out. Focus your eyes on some point straight ahead to help maintain your balance. Place a chair in front of you for assisted balance.

83 ADDUCTOR LIFT

HIP MUSCLES

◀ Wrap each ankle with a 5- or 10-lb. ankle weight. Lie on one side with both legs extended. Extend the arm and rest the head on it. Bend the knee of the top leg, and place the foot on the floor behind the opposite knee. Flex the foot of the straight leg.

▶ Slowly raise the leg four to six inches. Hold for a two-second count and slowly return to the start position. Do not let the leg rest. Repeat up to 15 reps. Do the same for the opposite side.

TIP Exercises 83, 84, and 85 strengthen the hips for more power and clubhead speed. Keep the toes and knee forward at all times.

84 BENT ABDUCTOR LIFT

HIP MUSCLES

◀ Lie on one side. Extend that arm to rest the head on it. Bend both knees and position the legs in a right angle. Hold a dumbbell in the other (opposite) hand and place the weight just above the knee.

▶ Lift the leg to just above hip level. Hold it there for a two-second count. Lower slowly to the start position. Do not rest the leg. Repeat up to 15 reps. Do the same for the opposite side.

TIP   Keep the leg in a right-angle position during the motion.

87 UPPER- AND LOWER-BODY PRONE LIFT

BACK MUSCLES

◀ Lie facedown with the legs extended, arms bent, and the hands under the chin for support. Flex (contract) the gluteals and upper-back muscles.

▶ Slowly lift the torso and both legs as high as possible. Hold for a two-second count and return to the start position. Do not let the feet or palms rest. Repeat up to 15 reps.

TIP   Keep the lower back relaxed.

88 BENT REVERSE ROW

BACK MUSCLES

Stand with your feet shoulder-width apart. Hold a dumbbell in each hand, with the palms facing away from the body. Bend forward until the body is just above parallel to the floor. Extend the arms down, and hold the weight in front of the knees about six inches away.

Flex the upper-back muscles and raise the weight upward toward the rib cage. Hold for a two-second count. Slowly return to the start position. Repeat up to 15 reps.

TIP Do not lift the torso during the motion.

89 ANGLED BICEPS CURL

UPPER-ARM MUSCLES

Sit on the end of the bench with both feet on the floor. Holding a dumbbell in each hand, position the elbows close to the rib cage. Extend the arms down and angle the weight away from the body.

Flex the biceps muscles and curl upward toward the shoulders. Hold for a two-second count. Return to the start position. Repeat up to 15 reps.

TIP For added distance off the tee, use exercises 89-92 to strengthen the upper arms and shoulders. Make sure you don't arch the back or make a rocking motion as you lift or lower the weight.

90 CONCENTRATION CURL

UPPER-ARM MUSCLES

Sit on the end of the bench. Holding a dumbbell in one hand, bend the torso and position the elbow to the inside of the knee.

Flex the biceps muscle and curl the weight upward toward the chin. Hold for a two-second count. Slowly return to the start position. Repeat up to 15 reps. Do the same for the opposite side.

TIP   Keep the elbow against the knee during the motion.

91 INCLINE CROSS EXTENSION

UPPER-ARM MUSCLES

Using the risers, elevate the platform to an incline position. Lie faceup on the bench with both feet on the floor. Holding a dumbbell in one hand, extend that arm up with the palm facing away from the body.

Bending the elbow, lower the weight to the opposite shoulder. Flex the triceps muscle and slowly return to the start position. Hold for a two-second count and repeat. Repeat up to 15 reps. Do the same for the opposite side.

TIP Do not swing the arm; keep the elbow pointed upward at all times.

92 TRICEPS DIP

UPPER-ARM MUSCLES

Sit at the center of the platform or the edge of a chair. Place both hands at each hip and grip the edge of the platform. Walk both feet away from the bench until the torso is just in front of the bench (and you are no longer sitting on the platform).

Bending the elbows, lower the torso until the elbows are just below parallel to the shoulders. Flex the triceps muscles and press upward. Hold for a two-second count. Repeat up to 15 reps.

TIP Do not press through the feet. **Recommendation:** You may feel the need to stretch before continuing. If so, repeat stretches 4 and 17.

93 FOREARM CURL

FOREARM, WRIST, AND HAND MUSCLES

Holding a dumbbell, position the elbow close to the rib cage. Bend the elbow to a right angle, with the forearm facing up.

Flex the forearm and curl the wrist upward. Hold for a two-second count. Return to the start position. Repeat up to 15 reps. Do the same for the opposite side.

TIP Use exercises 93 and 94 to improve club control. Do not lift the forearm during the motion.

94 WRIST CURL

FOREARM, WRIST, AND HAND MUSCLES

Holding a dumbbell, position the elbow close to the rib cage. Bend the elbow to a right angle, with the forearm facing down.

Flex the forearm and curl the wrist upward. Hold for a two-second count. Return to the start position. Repeat up to 15 reps. Do the same for the opposite side.

TIP Do not lift the forearm during the motion.

95 FRONT REVERSE LATERAL

SHOULDER MUSCLES

◀ Stand with the feet shoulder-width apart. Holding a dumbbell in each hand, extend the arms down.

◀ Lift both arms upward to shoulder height.

▶ Pull both weights backward, forming a right angle with the arms. Hold for a two-second count. Push the weight forward to shoulder height. Slowly return to the start position. Repeat up to 15 reps.

TIP Perform exercises 95 and 96 to increase stability at the top of the backswing. Do not arch the back or make a rocking motion as you lift and lower the weight.

96 BENT SHOULDER LATERAL

SHOULDER MUSCLES

Sit on the end of the bench or in a chair with both feet on the floor. Holding a dumbbell in each hand, extend the arms down to the side. Bend at the waist until the torso is just above parallel to the floor.

Slowly raise both arms outward until the arms are parallel to the floor. Hold for a two-second count. Return to the start position. Repeat up to 15 reps.

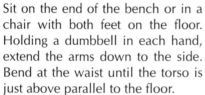 **TIP**   Do not arch the back or lift the torso during the motion.

97 MODIFIED PUSH-UPS

CHEST MUSCLES

◀ Place the hands on the floor, shoulder-width apart; place the knees on the floor, and elevate the lower legs. Tilt the torso forward until the shoulders, torso, and buttocks (in a straight line) form a 45-degree angle with the floor.

▶ Lower the torso toward the floor. Hold for a two-second count and slowly return to the start position, flexing the pectoral muscles. Repeat up to 15 reps.

TIP To maximize effectiveness in the golf swing, perform exercises 97, 98, and 99. Keep the head in a neutral position and do not arch the back.

98 ADVANCED PUSH-UPS

CHEST MUSCLES

◀ Place the hands on the floor, shoulder-width apart, and extend both legs back. Elevate both feet atop the platform.

▶ Lower the torso toward the floor. Hold for a two-second count and slowly return to the start position, flexing the pectoral muscles. Repeat up to 15 reps.

TIP   Keep the head in a neutral position and do not arch the back.

99 INCLINE CHEST FLY

CHEST MUSCLES

Using the risers, elevate the platform to an incline position. Lie faceup on the bench with both feet on the floor. Hold a dumbbell in each hand and extend the arms upward. Bend the elbows slightly, as though hugging a barrel.

Flex (contract) the pectoral muscles and slowly lower the weight out and down until the elbows are just below parallel to the bench. Hold for a two-second count and then slowly return to the start position. Repeat up to 15 reps.

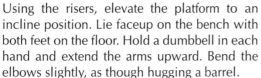
TIP   Relax the grip during the motion; do not arch the back while lifting. **Recommendation:** You may feel the need to stretch before continuing. If so, repeat stretches 6, 7, and 17.

100 LOWER-ABDOMINALS EXTENSION

ABDOMINAL MUSCLES

◀ Sit at one end of the bench and grip the sides with both hands. Bending the knees, raise both legs toward the chest.

▶ Flex the abdominal muscles, extend the legs straight out, and at the same time lie back on the platform. Hold for a two-second count. Repeat up to 15 reps.

TIP Strengthen your abdominals to improve posture at address with exercises 100-103. Do not raise the torso by pushing with the hands.

101 SIDE OBLIQUES

ABDOMINAL MUSCLES

◀ Lie back on the floor with both knees bent and your feet flat on the floor. Place the hands behind the head for neck support. Lower the knees to one side.

▶ Flex the abdominal muscles and slowly curl upward until the shoulders are off the floor. Hold for a two-second count and then return to the start position. Repeat up to 15 reps. Do the same for the opposite side.

TIP Use the abdomen to lift. Do not strain your neck.

102 OBLIQUES REACH

ABDOMINAL MUSCLES

◀ Lie back on the floor with both knees bent and your heels on the floor. Place one hand behind the head for support and extend the opposite arm, placing the hand at midthigh.

▶ Flex the abdomen and curl the torso upward and to one side until your palm reaches the knee. Hold for a two-second count and return to the start position. Repeat up to 15 reps. Do the same for the opposite side.

TIP   Use the abdomen to lift. Do not strain your neck.   •

103 BICYCLE CRUNCH

ABDOMINAL MUSCLES

◀ Lie back on the floor with the legs bent and forming a right angle; place both hands behind the head for support.

▶ Curl the torso upward; cross one elbow across the body while pulling the opposite knee inward toward the chest. Return to the start position and then repeat for the opposite side. Repeat up to 15 reps each side.

TIP Maintain a slow fluid motion.

Partner-Assisted Flexibility and Strength Exercises

Chapter 2 emphasizes static stretching to improve your flexibility. But if you have access to a partner or a trainer to assist you there is a more effective way to stretch. It's called PNF stretching (short for proprioceptive neuromuscular facilitation) and it allows you to stretch farther than you would normally be able to on your own, which increases your range of motion. While this technique increases the potential benefits of stretching it also increases the risk of injury; therefore you should take a cautious approach and work slowly using this method. The PNF method can be effective regardless of your fitness level but it is best added as part of the poststretch routine. Substitute PNF stretches for some of the exercises you chose in chapter 2.

Strength training with a partner also has added benefits. A trainer or a training partner helps keep you motivated and gives you the opportunity to focus on improving your exercise technique and the pace of the workout. If you are helping someone else train, be aware of their individual strengths and weaknesses. It's important to position yourself properly during each exercise so that you're able to assist your partner if needed.

When stretching with a partner, make sure to communicate. The person stretching should always signal when he or she feels a good stretch. Stretch to the point of gain, not to the point of pain. Encourage relaxation and proper breathing technique.

You will find partner-assisted flexibility exercises on pages 126-149, and partner-assisted strength exercises on pages 150-160.

104 TILT STRETCH

NECK MUSCLES

Sit on a bench or in a chair, with your arms at your sides. Flexing or contracting the abdominal muscles to support the back, be sure to sit upright.

Slowly drop the head toward one shoulder. Return to the start position. Repeat to the opposite side.

TRAINER Stand behind your client. Gently apply pressure from the top of the head to accelerate the stretch. The opposite hand should be on the shoulder to prevent the client from lifting. Repeat to the opposite side. Ensure that your client is relaxed and breathing properly.

105 SEATED TRICEPS STRETCH

ARM MUSCLES

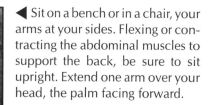

◀ Sit on a bench or in a chair, your arms at your sides. Flexing or contracting the abdominal muscles to support the back, be sure to sit upright. Extend one arm over your head, the palm facing forward.

◀ Bend the extended arm and slowly drop down the palm.

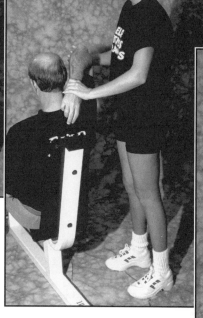

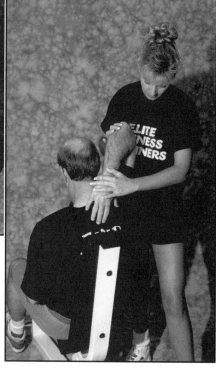

TRAINER Stand beside your client. Apply downward pressure to the wrist while pressing against the upper arm to accelerate the stretch. Repeat to the opposite side. Ensure that your client is relaxed and breathing properly.

106 STANDING TRICEPS STRETCH

ARM MUSCLES

Stand with your feet shoulder-width apart and your arms by your sides. Extend one arm, the palm facing forward, above your head.

Bend the extended arm, and slowly drop it down.

TRAINER	Stand behind your client. Apply downward pressure to the wrist while pressing against the upper arm to accelerate the stretch. Repeat for the opposite side. Ensure that your client is relaxed and breathing properly.
TIP	If you are stretching your client on the course, use a club for assistance. Gently pull the club downward to accelerate the stretch. Keep the club close to the body to ensure there is no arching of the back.

107 RIB CAGE STRETCH

ARM AND SHOULDER MUSCLES

Sit on a bench or in a chair. Flexing or contracting the abdominal muscles to support the back, be sure to sit upright. Extend the arms upward and press the palms together as shown.

Stretch the arms up and slightly backward.

TRAINER Stand behind your client. Accelerate the stretch by gently pulling upward from just above the elbow. Ensure that your client is relaxed, breathing properly, and not arching the back.

108 BACK OF SHOULDER STRETCH

ARM AND SHOULDER MUSCLES

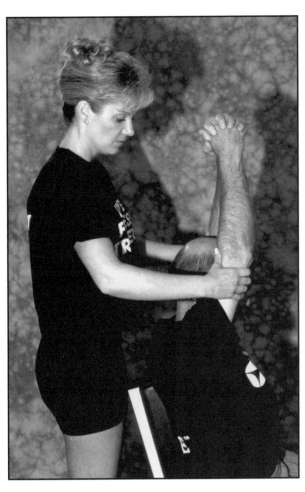
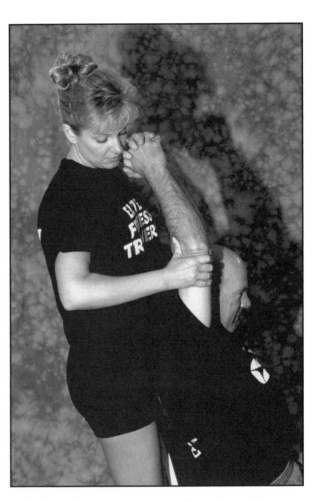

Sit on a bench or in a chair. Flexing or contracting the abdominal muscles to support the back, be sure to sit upright. Interlace the fingers above the head as shown.

With the palms facing downward, gently push the arms back and up.

TRAINER Stand behind your client. Accelerate the stretch by gently pulling upward from just above the elbow. Ensure that your client is relaxed, breathing properly, and not arching the back.

109 FRONT OF SHOULDER AND CHEST STRETCH

ARM AND SHOULDER MUSCLES

Stand with the feet shoulder-width apart and the toes pointing straight ahead.

Extend the arms down and back. Inhale and slowly expand the chest. To accelerate the stretch, lift the arms upward.

TRAINER Stand behind your client. Accelerate the stretch by encompassing both arms and gently pressing together. Ensure that your client is relaxed, breathing properly, and not arching the back.

110 MIDBACK STRETCH

ARM AND SHOULDER MUSCLES

Stand with one arm at your side and the other extended forward.

Gently pull the arm across the chest toward the opposite shoulder. Return to the start position and repeat for the opposite side.

TRAINER Stand behind your client. Place one hand on the client's wrist and the opposite hand on the shoulder to prevent the client from turning the torso. Accelerate the stretch by gently pulling the arm across the chest. Repeat to the opposite side.

111 ROTATION STRETCH

UPPER-TRUNK MUSCLES

Stand with your feet shoulder-width apart and your arms extended in front of you.

As the trainer rotates you, slowly turn your upper body as far as possible—with only minimal turn in your hips.

TRAINER   Hold the wrists of your client. Slowly rotate the individual. Accelerate the stretch by gently rotating the client as far as possible without the hips turning. Ensure that his feet remain in the start position. To keep the client's arms in proper position, use a club to position the arms shoulder-width apart. Repeat to the opposite side.

112 CALF STRETCH

LOWER-LEG MUSCLES

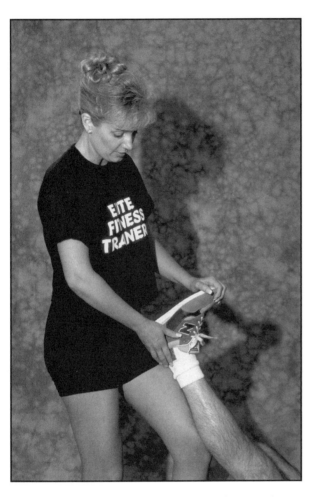

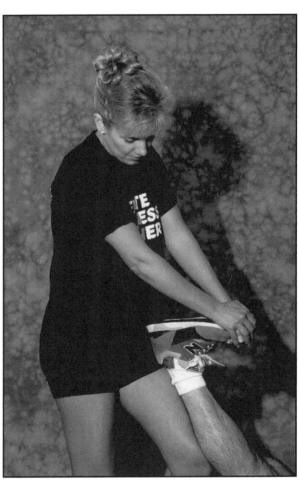

Lie on your back on the floor and lift one leg straight up.

Flex the foot on the lifted leg and stretch it toward you.

TRAINER Place one of the client's feet on your upper thigh. Flex the foot and accelerate the stretch by gently applying pressure to the ball of the foot. Repeat to the opposite side.

113 SHIN STRETCH

LOWER-LEG MUSCLES

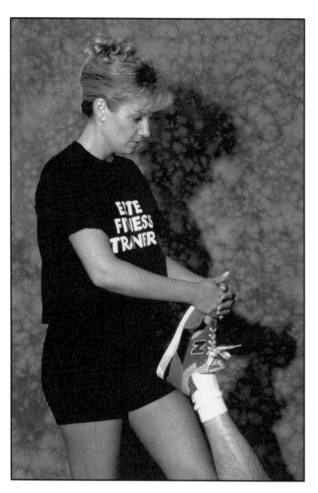

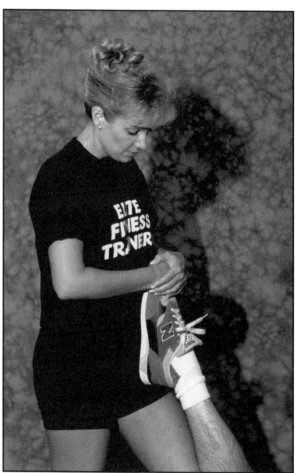

Lie on your back on the floor and lift one leg straight up.

Flex the lifted foot and extend it away from you.

TRAINER From the same position as the calf stretch, accelerate the stretch by gently pulling back from the top of the foot. Repeat to the opposite side.

114 PRAY STRETCH

SHOULDER, ARM, AND BACK MUSCLES

◀ Position yourself on your hands and knees.

▼ Reach forward with your hands 12 to 14 inches, keeping your palms on the floor. Slowly pull back while you continue to press downward with your palms. Let your chest drop slightly toward the floor to accelerate the stretch. Return to the start position.

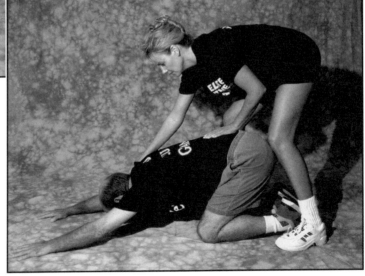

TRAINER Stand behind your client to prevent the individual's sitting back too far. Accelerate the stretch by gently applying pressure to the top of the back and pressing downward. Ensure that your client is relaxed and breathing properly.

115 CAT STRETCH

SHOULDER, ARM, AND BACK MUSCLES

Position yourself on your hands and knees.

Slowly round your back upward until you feel a good stretch. Return to the start position.

TRAINER From the same position as the pray stretch, accelerate the stretch by placing one hand on the client's abdomen and gently pressing upward. This assist also ensures that the client does not drop the abdomen quickly as he or she relaxes the stretch.

116 LATS AND BACK STRETCH

SHOULDER, ARM, AND BACK MUSCLES

Position yourself on your hands and knees.

Place your hands to one side, reaching away from the body with the outward arm, and slowly rotate your torso creating the stretch. Return to the start position and repeat to the opposite side.

TRAINER Stand behind your client. Place one hand on the hip and the opposite hand on the back to ensure that your client does not shift the hip outward while stretching. Repeat to the opposite side.

117 BICEPS, FOREARMS, AND WRISTS STRETCH

ARM MUSCLES

Position yourself on your hands and knees. Slowly rotate your wrists until your thumbs are pointed to the outside with your fingers pointed toward your knees.

Keeping your palms flat, lean back until you feel a good stretch. Return to the start position.

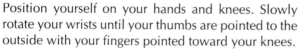

TRAINER Kneel to one side of your client. Place one hand at the base of the back. This will give you the vantage point to ensure your client does not lift the palms or overreach on the stretch.

118 FRONT HIP STRETCH

HIP MUSCLES

Begin on your knees and move one leg forward until the knee of this forward leg is directly over the ankle.

Leaning forward, then lower the front of your hip downward to create the stretch. Return to the start position and repeat to the opposite side.

TRAINER	Kneel to one side of your client. Join interior hands: this assists your client with balance and ensures proper positioning. Repeat to the opposite side.
TIP	If your client has knee problems, place padding beneath the knee.

119 HAMSTRINGS STRETCH

HIP AND LOWER-BACK MUSCLES

Sit on the floor or ground with your legs straight, no more than six inches apart, and your feet upright.

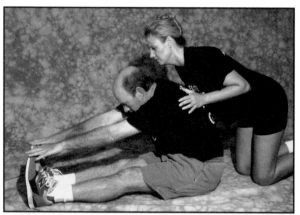

Bend from the waist and reach forward to create the stretch. Return to the start position.

If you are stretching on the course, stand with your arms folded, and bend at the waist.

TRAINER	Kneel behind your client and place both hands on the upper back. Accelerate the stretch by gently pressing forward.
TIP	If you are stretching your client on the course, you can simulate the same stretch by having the client bend at the waist. To ensure proper speed and position, have your client fold the arms; you should contact the client just above the elbows.

120 LYING QUADS STRETCH

HIP AND UPPER-LEG MUSCLES

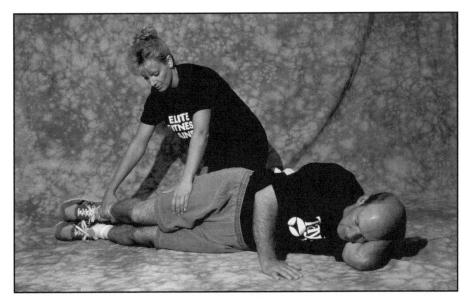

◀ Lie on one side and rest your head on your arm. Bend the knee of your top leg.

▶ As the trainer pulls the heel toward the buttock, contract the buttock and push the hip forward to create the stretch.

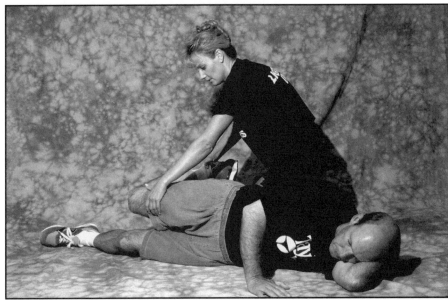

TRAINER Kneel behind your client. Place one hand on the client's upper thigh and the opposite hand atop the foot. Accelerate the stretch by gently pulling the foot toward the buttock. Repeat to the opposite side.

121 LOWER-BACK STRETCH

SPINE

Lie faceup with your knees bent and feet flat on the floor.

Pull one leg toward your chest, keeping your head on the floor.

TRAINER Place one hand under the client's knee and the opposite hand on the heel of the foot. Accelerate the stretch by gently pressing downward on the thigh. Repeat to the opposite side. Ensure that your client is relaxed and breathing properly.

122 LOW HIP STRETCH

SPINE

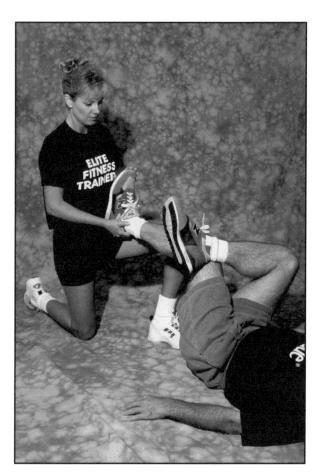

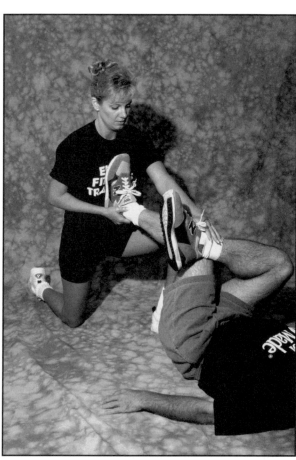

Lie on your back with your knees bent and feet flat on the floor. Cross one leg, placing your ankle just above the knee of the opposite leg.

Create the stretch by pulling the crossed leg toward you.

TRAINER Put your client in the start position. Holding the ankle and the top of the foot, lift the leg to a position parallel to the floor. Place the bottom of the foot against your chest and place one hand at the crossed ankle. Accelerate the stretch by pressing forward. Repeat to the opposite side.

123 HIP AND THIGH STRETCH

SPINE

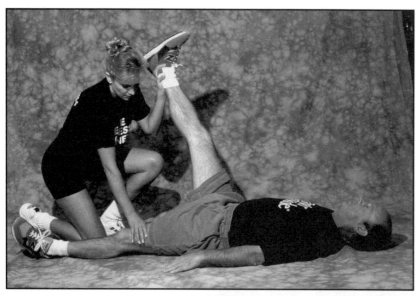

◀ Lie on your back with the legs extended in front and arms by your sides. Lift one leg straight up.

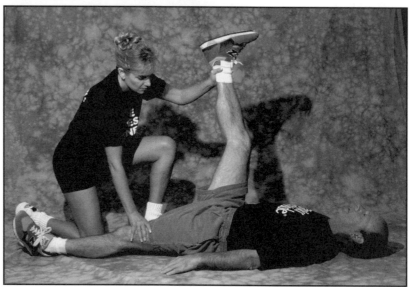

▶ Create the stretch by pulling the lifted leg toward you.

TRAINER Hold one ankle and place the opposite hand on the thigh. Accelerate the stretch by gently lifting the leg upward and toward the client's chest. Apply downward pressure on the thigh. Repeat to the opposite side.

124 SIDE HIP STRETCH

LOWER-TRUNK MUSCLES

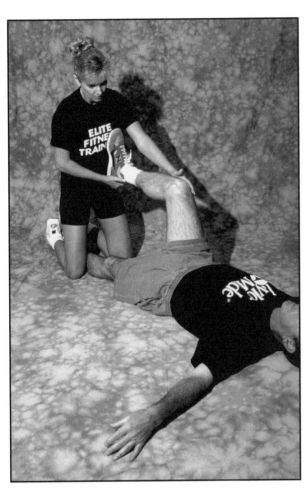

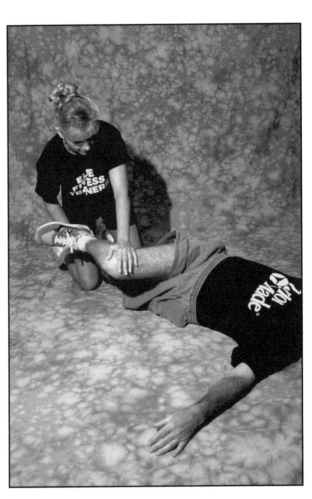

Lie on your back with the legs extended and arms outstretched. Bend one knee at 90 degrees and lower it to the opposite side.

As the trainer presses the knee downward, turn your head toward the opposite side.

TRAINER Straddle one leg and position the opposite leg in a 90-degree angle holding the ankle. Place the opposite hand on the outside of the client's knee. Accelerate the stretch by gently pressing the bent knee downward. Ensure that your client's shoulders remain on the floor. Repeat to the opposite side.

125 BUTTOCKS STRETCH

LOWER-TRUNK MUSCLES

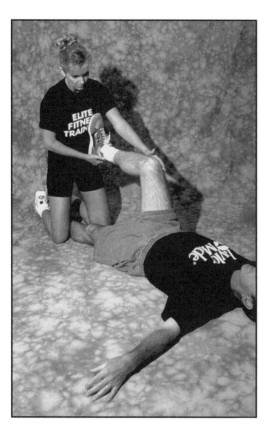

Position yourself as in the side hip stretch. As the trainer presses the leg upward, turn your head toward the opposite side.

TRAINER From the side hip stretch, extend the leg holding the ankle. Accelerate the stretch by gently pressing upward toward the client's shoulder. Repeat to the opposite side.

126 GROIN STRETCH

INNER-THIGH MUSCLES

Lie on your back with the knees bent. Lower the legs toward the ground in this bent position, placing the soles of the feet together.

The pull of gravity creates the stretch.

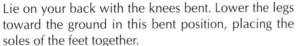

TRAINER Place both hands on the outside of the thighs. Gently lower the legs to a comfortable position. Accelerate the stretch by placing both hands just above the knees and apply gentle downward pressure.

127 ABS AND ANKLES STRETCH

ABDOMINAL AND ANKLE MUSCLES

Lie on your back with the legs extended and arms outstretched above your head.

Reach as far as you can in the opposite direction with your arms and legs (point your toes and extend your fingers) until you feel a good stretch.

TRAINER   Place both hands atop the feet. Accelerate the stretch by applying downward pressure as the client reaches overhead.

128 ADVANCED LUNGE

UPPER-LEG MUSCLES

◀ Stand with your feet together at a comfortable distance from a platform. Hold a dumbbell in each hand and extend the arms down.

◀ Extend one foot forward, placing it atop the platform.

▶ At the same time, bend the knee of the opposite leg. Moving in a downward motion, lift the heel of the opposite leg. Spring back to the start position by pressing through the heel of the front foot.

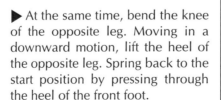

TRAINER Stand at one end of the platform. This allows you to prevent your client from leaning forward and to assist him or her with balance.

129 INTERMEDIATE SQUAT

UPPER-LEG MUSCLES

Stand with the feet shoulder-width apart. Hold a dumbbell in each hand and extend the arms down.

Descend to a squatting position, keeping the knees directly above the toes. Squat to a 45-degree bend in the knees. Hold for a two-second count and slowly rise to the start position.

TRAINER Stand behind your client and place your hands on the individual's waist. This allows you to assist your client with balance and to prevent him or her from leaning forward.

130 STRAIGHT CALF

LOWER-LEG MUSCLES

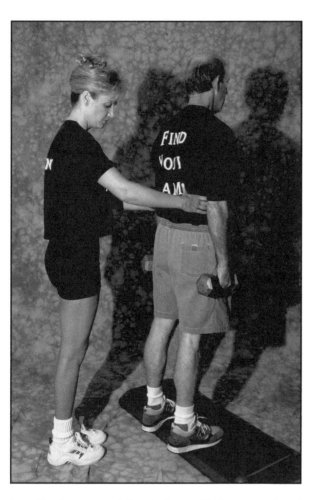

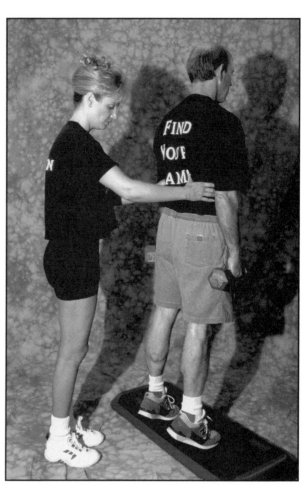

Stand in the center of the platform with the toes pointed straight ahead. Move both feet back until the heels are off the platform. Hold a dumbbell in each hand and extend the arms down.

Raise both heels as high as possible flexing the calf muscles. Hold for a two-second count and return to the start position.

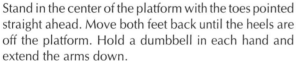

TRAINER Stand behind your client and place your hands on the individual's waist. This allows you to assist your client with balance.

131 HAMMER BICEPS CURL

UPPER-ARM MUSCLES

Sit in a chair or on a bench with both feet flat on the floor. Holding a dumbbell in each hand, extend the arms down to the sides.

Keep the weight in a "hammer" position, flex the biceps, and curl one arm upward toward the shoulder. As the weight approaches the shoulder, flex the opposite biceps and begin curling the opposite arm. Lower the weight that first began curling as the opposite arm ascends.

TRAINER Kneel behind your client and place your hands on the biceps. This allows you to ensure that the elbows stay in proper position.

132 ANGLED BICEPS CURL

UPPER-ARM MUSCLES

Sit in a chair or on a bench with both feet on the floor. Hold a dumbbell in each hand and place the elbows close to the rib cage. Extend the arms down and angle the weight away from the body.

Flex the biceps muscles and curl the arms upward toward shoulders. Hold for a two-second count.

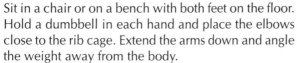

TRAINER Kneel behind your client and place your hands on the biceps. This allows you to ensure that the elbows stay in proper position.

133 SEATED SHOULDER LATERALS

SHOULDER MUSCLES

Sit on a bench with your feet on the floor. Hold a dumbbell in each hand and extend the arms down at the sides.

Then raise both arms upward until the wrists are just above shoulder height. Hold for a two-second count and slowly return to the start position.

TRAINER   Stand behind your client to ensure that the weight is lifted properly.

134 SIMULTANEOUS FRONT LATERALS/ FRONT REVERSE LATERALS

ARM AND SHOULDER MUSCLES

◀ Stand with the feet shoulder-width apart. Hold a dumbbell in each hand with the arms extended down.

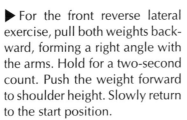

◀ Lift both arms upward to shoulder height. Hold for a two-second count and slowly return to the start position. This is the simultaneous front lateral.

▶ For the front reverse lateral exercise, pull both weights backward, forming a right angle with the arms. Hold for a two-second count. Push the weight forward to shoulder height. Slowly return to the start position.

TRAINER Stand to one side of your client to assist the person with proper form. Stand behind your client, however, when assisting with the front reverse (shown in the third photo) to ensure that your client does not pass the point of parallel.

135 MILITARY PUSH-UPS

CHEST MUSCLES

◀ Place the hands on the floor, shoulder-width apart, and extend both legs back.

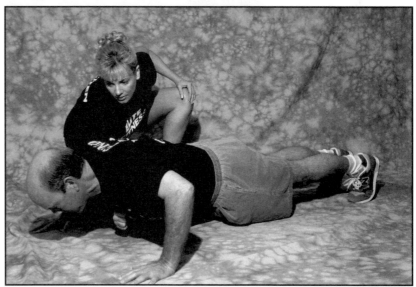

▶ Lower the torso toward the floor. Hold for a two-second count and slowly return to the start position, flexing (contracting) the pectoral muscles.

TRAINER Kneel to one side of your client and ensure that the client has proper form during the exercise.

136 FLAT CROSS EXTENSIONS

UPPER-ARM MUSCLES

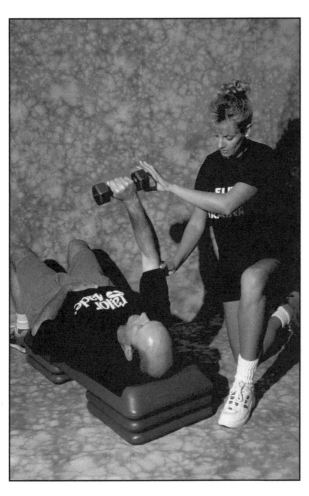 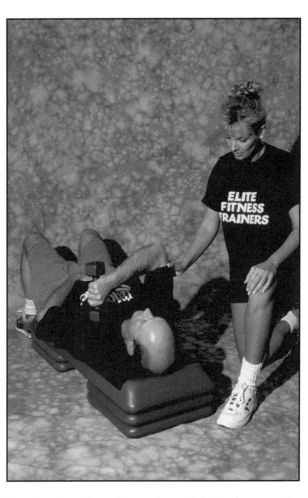

Lie faceup on the platform with both feet on the floor. Hold a dumbbell in one hand and extend the arm up, with the palm facing away from the body.

Bending the elbow, lower the weight to the opposite shoulder. Flex the triceps muscle and slowly return to the start position. Hold for a two-second count and repeat.

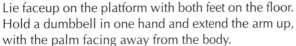

TRAINER Kneel to one side of your client and place your hands to ensure that the person's elbow stays in proper position during the exercise.

137 REVERSE EXTENSIONS

UPPER-ARM MUSCLES

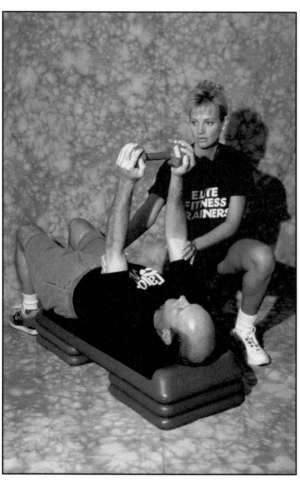
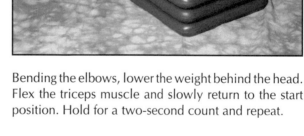

Lie faceup on the platform with both feet on the floor. Hold a dumbbell with both hands, gripping the outside heads of the dumbbell. Extend both arms upward and slightly back over the head.

Bending the elbows, lower the weight behind the head. Flex the triceps muscle and slowly return to the start position. Hold for a two-second count and repeat.

TRAINER Kneel to one side of your client to place your hands so as to ensure that the elbows stay in proper position during the exercise.

138 ASSISTED OBLIQUES

ABDOMINAL MUSCLES

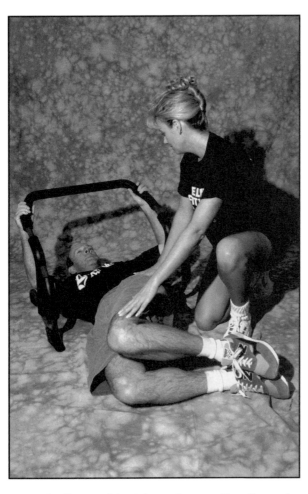

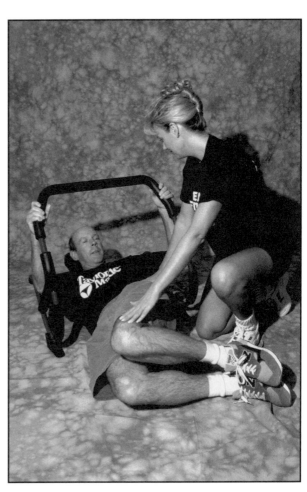

Lie on the floor with both knees bent and feet flat on the floor. Rest the head and arms in the ab roller. Lower the knees to one side.

Flex the abdominal muscles and slowly curl upward until the shoulders are off the floor. Hold for a two-second count and return to the start position.

TRAINER Kneel to one side of your client and place your hand on the obliques; this allows you to ensure that the client is executing the exercise properly.

about the author

Kelly Blackburn

Since 1994, Kelly Blackburn has been the fitness consultant and personal fitness trainer for players on both the PGA TOUR and Senior PGA TOUR. She has worked closely with Fred Couples, Larry Nelson, Dave Stockton, Hubert Green, Bob Duval, Hale Irwin, and many others. She is also the creator and host of the PGA TOUR Fitness Center featured on pgatour.com.

Blackburn is president of Elite Personal Fitness Trainers, which specializes in locating fitness professionals to assist players with their fitness goals. She is also a fitness columnist for *GolfLife Magazine* and is on the advisory board for MET-Rx Nutrition. She has been developing specialized fitness programs to help individuals achieve their fitness goals for more than a decade.

Blackburn lives in Atlanta, Georgia.